Sándor Ferenczi:
Reconsidering Active Intervention

This is the first study in English of one of the first generation of psychoanalysts – a member of Freud's inner circle, founder and President of the International Psycho-Analytical Association, the analyst of Melanie Klein, Michael Balint, Ernest Jones, and a highly original analytic thinker. Martin Stanton provides a chronology of Ferenczi's life and work, followed by a series of reflections on his writings with particular emphasis on his contributions to training, teaching and psychoanalytic technique, sexuality and child sexual abuse, and Ferenczi's experiments with the boundaries of the relations between patient and analyst. A cloud – largely created by Jones – has hung over Ferenczi's work, especially its closing stages. Stanton's book is more than an introduction: it invites us to give Ferenczi his proper status as a pioneer whose ideas have wide and deep current relevance.

Martin Stanton is the Director of the Centre for Psychoanalytic Studies at the University of Kent and is the author of *Outside the Dream: Lacan and French Styles of Psychoanalysis.*

Sándor Ferenczi:
Reconsidering
Active Intervention

Sándor Ferenczi: Reconsidering Active Intervention

MARTIN STANTON

Jason Aronson Inc.
Northvale, New Jersey | London

10 9 8 7 6 5 4 3 2 1

Library of Congress Cataloging-in-Publication Data

Stanton, Martin, 1950–
    Sándor Ferenczi : reconsidering active intervention / by Martin
Stanton.
      p. cm
    Includes bibliographical references and index.
    ISBN 0-87668-569-6.—ISBN 1-85343-136-2 (Free Association Books
: cased).—ISBN 1-85343-137-0 (Free Association Books : pbk.)
    1. Ferenczi, Sándor, 1873–1933. 2. Psychiatrists—Hungary—
Biography. 3. Psychoanalysts—Hungary—Biography. I. Title.
    [DNLM: 1. Ferenczi, Sándor, 1873–1933. 2. Psychoanalysis—
biography. WZ 100 F349S]
RC438.6.F47S73   1991
616.89'0092—dc20
[B]
DNLM/DLC
for Library of Congress   90-14523

Manufactured in the United States of America. Jason Aronson Inc. offers books and cassettes. For information and catalog write to Jason Aronson Inc., 230 Livingston Street, Northvale, New Jersey 07647.

IN MEMORY OF MY MOTHER

Yg koet ymaes ym bro ym bryn
canhwyll yn tywyll a gerd genhyn

(In forest and on plain, on hill and dale,
a candle in the darkness goes with us)

Dafydd ap Gwilym

Contents

NOTE ON ABBREVIATED REFERENCES
USED IN TEXT

The English Ferenczi references will indicate one of the following volumes plus page numbers: Volume 1 *First Contributions to Psycho-Analysis* (Hogarth Press, 1952); Volume 2 *Further Contributions to the Theory and Technique of Psycho-Analysis* (Hogarth Press, 1926); Volume 3 *Final Contributions to the Problems and Methods of Psycho-Analysis* (Hogarth Press, 1955); so, for example, the abbreviated reference in the text for Volume 2, p. 151, will read: Ferenczi, 2, p. 151.

Similarly, the German Ferenczi references will indicate the following volume numbers: Volume 1 *Theorie* (Internationaler Psychoanalytischer Verlag, 1927); Volume 2 *Praxis* (Internationaler Psychoanalytischer Verlag, 1927); Volume 3 *Arbeiten aus den Jahren 1908–1933* (Huber, 1939); Volume 4 *Gedenkartikel, Kritiken und Referate, Fragmente* (Huber, 1939). This will be prefaced by *Bausteine*; so, for example, the abbreviated reference in the text for Volume 3, p. 271, will read: Ferenczi, *Bausteine*, 3, p. 271.

Where the title of the individual paper by Ferenczi is relevant to the text, this will also be included. References to Ferenczi's *Thalassa: A Theory of Genitality* (Maresfield/ Karnac, [1924] 1989) will be abbreviated in the text to: Ferenczi, *Thalassa*, followed by the page number. References to the *Clinical Diary* (Harvard, 1988) will take the form: *Diary*, p. 22. References to the *Ferenczi/Groddeck Correspondence 1921–1933* (Payot, 1982) will appear in the text as: Ferenczi and Groddeck, p. 135.

All references to Freud refer to the date recorded and the appropriate volume number of the *Standard Edition* so that, e.g., 'Obsessions and phobias', volume 3, p. 71, will feature in the text as: Freud, 1895c, 3, p. 71. Again the title of the paper will be given if it is especially relevant to the text. Similarly, reference to the work of Jung will be to the *Collected Works* and be given in the form of volume number followed by page number (e.g., Jung, 1923, 6, p. 67) and references to Ernest Jones's *Life and Work of Sigmund Freud* will also appear as volume number followed by page number, e.g., Jones, 3, p. 98. For further details of both, see the bibliography.

Acknowledgements

Some of the most positive and the most negative transferences occur in reading, and some of the most subtle forms of censorship operate through intellectual debate. So those embarking on a critical exposition of a person's written work should be careful to check their own responses, if necessary by long critical looks in the mirror, aided by frank advice from personal advocates. To some extent, naturally, expositional fervour will cloud supposed academic clarity with numerous layers of identification. We can project into any textual body whatever we wish; and we can then introject most of the disappointment derived from what the textual body failed to reveal. We can also check the academic mirror to find out what is reflected in the flash, or feed-back, of interpretation. So, starting right here, this book acknowledges the primary role of the unconscious.

Second, it should be added that this particular critical project is not exclusively critical. It aims to challenge the kind of distinction between theory and practice that much psychoanalysis has previously sought to enforce. Analytical training bodies, for example, are often embarrassed by academic discourses – whether they be historical, philosophical or aesthetic. Instead, they privilege the concrete – the clinical case and its supervision – imagining that it is separate from the other discourses. Likewise, the academic continuously redesigns the ivory-tower ethic, privileging distance from practical concerns, worries or bodily feelings. There is no need, for example, ever to meet, live with or work with schizophrenics to be able to appraise their art.

This book has been written across such divides. It was conceived during lectures and seminars in the psychoanalytic studies programme at the University of Kent. It also reflects clinical practice, with all its very special narratives. The writing of what the reader reads here, therefore, has been interspersed with comments on essays, case notes and assessment of supervision. I hope this is evident. In any case, I have derived much from this contrast in writing this book.

Researching and writing on Ferenczi have proved particularly appropriate and useful for me. Ferenczi's attempts to establish 'psychoanalytic studies' as a university subject in its own right have been a constant inspiration while I have been engaged in the founding of the Kent Psychoanalytic Studies Centre. In my clinical work, too, I have derived great benefit in working with borderline patients from reading through Ferenczi's doubts about and revisions of 'active technique'. This has particularly helped me to clarify the problem of if, when and how, one should 'actively' intervene and provide interpretative structures for those who are incapable of providing their own and therefore demand some practical advice.

Obviously, I assume that identification, transference and countertransference are continuously at play here, and I have tried, where possible, to incorporate them in the text, if not in the structure of the text. These factors simply emphasize the mutual basis of this work. To mention but a few names, I offer thanks to: my patients; the students and staff of the Centre for Psychoanalytic Studies, University of Kent; Richard Wells, Michael Molnar and the staff at the Freud Museum, London, for help with the Freud/Ferenczi Correspondence; Leslie Hall and Julia Shepherd at the Melanie Klein Trust, Wellcome Library, London, for help with Melanie Klein's papers; Jill Duncan, Librarian at the Institute of Psycho-Analysis, London, for access to Ferenczi's German publications; Miranda Chaytor, for help with the manuscript.

A number of friends and colleagues have provided stimulating and valuable criticism: Bernard Burgoyne, Gilles Chouraqui, Karl Figlio, Hugh Freeman, Jim Gollnick, Meira Likierman, Brian Morton, Michael Parsons, Andrew Paskauskas, Malcolm Pines, Sonu Shamdasani and Alex Tarnopolski. I owe a special debt to Jean Laplanche, the effects of whose insights are very evident here.

I would also like to thank the following close friends and relatives for their support: Victoria Armstrong-Totten, Pam and Brian Doherty, Susan Fowler, Camilla and Curtis Jones, Erika Lehner, Lauchlan Munro, Richard Rooke, Casper Sinnege, and Harry, Terry and Luce Stanton. Bob Young has been an inspiration in nourishing social change without selling out. His ideas and criticisms have been greatly appreciated.

I feel a very special gratitude to the following: my father, for his constant support; my nephew, Simon, for sharing the true story of Humpty-Dumpty; and finally, my wife, Kristina, who has not only loved, lived with and supported me, but shared these thoughts and taught me much.

Martin Stanton
Canterbury, March 1990

Metabasis

WHY BEGIN TO read and study Ferenczi? There are a few obvious reasons: his position as founder and former President of the IPA (International Psycho-Analytical Association); his pioneer role in formulating training programmes for psychoanalysts; his innovative role in reforming psychoanalytic technique and proposing more flexibility and 'active' intervention by the analyst; his contribution to the debate on possible psychoanalytic treatment for victims of child sex abuse; his subtle defence of 'lay', or non-medical, psychoanalysis against powerful and vociferous opposition in the United States; finally, his close friendship and co-operation with all the founders of psychoanalysis, especially Freud and Jung, with whom he travelled to the United States in 1909.

None the less, despite all this, there is surprisingly little critical appreciation of his importance. Why? It is tempting, first of all, to blame character assassination. The circulation of pernicious rumours that Ferenczi was deranged and seduced patients hardly encouraged serious study of his work. The source of many of these rumours was Ernest Jones, who seriously libelled Ferenczi in *The Life and Work of Sigmund Freud*. Jones claimed, falsely, that Ferenczi lapsed into a severe psychosis during the last years of his life, and this discredited all Ferenczi's later work. In fact, right from the start, Jones's accusations were contended and dismissed (cf. Fromm, 1963, pp. 94ff.; Roazen, 1979; Masson, 1984, pp. 145ff.; Dupont, 1988; Gay, 1988). Critics have been quick to suggest either that Jones still harboured negative transference feelings for Ferenczi, who was his analyst, or that he was simply miffed by Ferenczi's less than flattering view of Jones's role in the development of psychoanalysis. However false such rumours may be, sadly they still tend to generate their own persuasive power. Even the most open-minded reader may yet pause and reflect before taking Ferenczi's volumes off the shelves.

More damaging to Ferenczi, perhaps, is the assumption that Freud actually condemned his 'active technique', with all its ramifications. There is no doubt that Freud sternly admonished Ferenczi for what he termed 'the kissing technique' (*Küsstechnik*), that is, the purported permission for patients to express physical affection to their analyst – as long, of course, as it did not drift into full-scale sexual intercourse. In fact, Freud's admonition was totally inappropriate, as neither active technique nor its variants, relaxation and mutual analysis, encouraged promiscuity between analyst and patient. Ferenczi argued rather that a deeply distressed patient sometimes needed to be held and comforted. To refuse to do so would be cruel and heartless. Of course, here again force of tradition tends to support Freud against Ferenczi, often regardless of the evidence.

One means of setting the record straight, and of vindicating Ferenczi, is a comprehensive study of archival sources and a careful critical appreciation of his published work. Unfortunately, the personal papers of many early psychoanalysts still remain inaccessible to the public, so extensive biographical research continues to be difficult, if not impossible. This book, therefore, opens with a 'curriculum vitae', which surveys the available biographical sources. It makes no pretence, however, of offering a definitive biography. That must wait for the future.

Another reason the psychoanalytic world seems largely to have overlooked Ferenczi is the lamentable state of the English edition of his work. Until his death in 1970, Michael Balint worked admirably to improve this, though against the tide of Jones's comments and, of course, the pressure of his own work. None the less, readers of the three English volumes of Ferenczi's 'contributions' to psychoanalysis will be struck by the quaint and often awkward prose and the absence of editorial provision of context and cross-reference. This book therefore attempts to comment on and clarify these editions. For this reason, there is close textual reference throughout, along with attention to the historical context in which Ferenczi's concepts developed. In this sense, the conceptual expositions here have been excogitated from the English translations.

If nothing else, this introduction hopes to inspire the reader to return to Ferenczi's work, to reread and reconsider it. Hopefully too, such a return implies a major re-evaluation of Ferenczi's importance for contemporary psychoanalysis. Significant here is the debt that 'object relations' theory owes to Ferenczi, a debt often readily admitted for one of his analysands, Michael Balint, but not for another, Melanie Klein. It will be suggested here that Kleinian 'play technique' drew major inspiration from Ferenczi's technical innovations and that her formulation of early infant development derived much from his teaching. Of course, as will be shown, there were significant differences, notably as Klein proceeded to define the 'depressive position', but these do not vitiate Ferenczi's critical influence.

Most important of all, the rediscovery of Ferenczi's innovations could inform problem areas in present psychoanalytic work: first, his pioneer work in teaching psychoanalysis as a university subject and his careful assessment of how far theoretical and practical aspects can pursue relatively independent objectives; second, his work in the diagnosis and treatment of child sex abuse: his notion of the 'languages of tenderness and passion' could prove extremely useful in clarifying the confusion of current debate; finally, his views on 'mutualism', which could inform new, co-operative ways of conceiving the analyst's interpretative intervention in the analytical session. This could help bridge the difference between perceptions of psychoanalysis as 'passive' and psychotherapy as 'active', and open up new space in the hybrid category of 'analytical psychotherapy'.

This book, then, aims both to restore Ferenczi to his rightful place at the centre of critical and historical debate on psychoanalysis and to indicate ways in which he might inspire future developments. As such, it follows the analogy of 'deferred action' (*Nachträglichkeit*): in the 'curriculum vitae' it presents a linear chronology of his life; then, in subsequent chapters, revisits major developmental stages to gain fresh insights. No matter how broad and drastic a revision of accepted opinion this may invite, it simply reiterates Ferenczi's original revolutionary fervour.

Curriculum Vitae

As long as one is satisfied with mere description, an exact tabulation of the details of a process is sufficient, and one is very easily able to confine oneself within one's own particular scientific boundaries. As soon, however, as one desires, in addition to description, to make some assertion regarding the meaning of a process, one involuntarily grasps for analogies in alien scientific fields.

Sándor Ferenczi—*Thalassa*, p. 3

1830

Bernath Fränkel, Ferenczi's father, is born in Krakov, Poland. In his teens he travels to Hungary, probably to escape anti-Semitic pogroms.

1840

Rósa Eibenschütz, Ferenczi's mother, is born in Krakov, Poland, on 11 December. The family move soon after to Vienna, Austria.

1848

Bernath Fränkel joins the patriotic forces opposing the Habsburg Empire's control of Hungary. These forces are quickly suppressed, but Fränkel decides to stay in Hungary and settles in the town of Miskolcz. He becomes manager of Michael Heilprin's bookshop in the centre of town and publishes and sells patriotic and radical literature. Later, he also becomes a part-time impresario, and invites prominent musicians, poets and speakers to Miskolcz.

1856

Sigmund Freud is born on 6 May in Freiberg, Moravia (now Pribor, Czechoslovakia). Michael Heilprin decides to return to his native America and Bernath Fränkel buys the bookshop from him.

1858

Bernath Fränkel and Rósa Eibenschütz marry in Vienna.

1866

Georg Groddeck is born on 13 October in Bad Kösen, Germany.

1868

Hungary adopts Hungarian as its official language. Previously, German had been used throughout the Habsburg Empire.

1873

Sándor Ferenczi is born on 7 July. He is the eighth of twelve children. The tenth, Vilma, died before she was a year old in 1881.

1875

Carl Gustav Jung is born on 26 July in Kesswil, Thurgau, Switzerland.

1879

The Fränkel family changes its name to the Hungarian 'Ferenczi'.

1888

Bernath Fränkel dies. According to Zsofia, the youngest daughter, Sándor was his favourite and used to accompany him regularly on his daily visits. The fifteen-year-old boy's mourning is accentuated by the fact that he receives 'too little love and too much severity' from his mother (Ferenczi to Groddeck, Christmas 1921, p. 55). Rósa takes over the running of the bookshop with great success, and later opens another branch in the neighbouring town of Nyiregyhàza. She is also President of the Union of Jewish Women in the area. Also at this time the family becomes closer to the Altschul family. Central to this is Gizella Altschul, who soon after marries Géza Pálos. They have two children, Elma and Magda. Magda later marries Sándor Ferenczi's younger brother, Lajos. Sándor himself is later to fall passionately in love with Gizella (whom in due course he marries) and then subsequently with Elma too, and this conflict haunts him for the rest of his life.

1893

After a distinguished career at Miskolcz's Protestant school, Sándor Ferenczi registers at the University of Vienna to read medicine. He stays with his uncle, Zsiga Fränkel, and sees a great deal of his favourite older brother Sigmund, who works as a chemist at a papermill in Bruck-an-der-Mur, near Vienna. The two brothers enjoy many mountain walks together. Later, Sigmund is reputed to have been the intermediary between Melanie Klein, the wife of his colleague Arthur Klein, and his brother Sándor. Sándor soon decides to specialize in neurology and psychiatry, and further develops his passion for hypnotism. In this context, he reads much French literature on hypnosis and hysteria, and comes across the work of Sigmund Freud for the first time ('Über den psychischen Mechanismus hysterischer Phänomene', with Breuer, in the *Neurologisches Zentralblatt*, January 1893). None the less, the main influence on him at this time is Max Schächter, editor of the medical journal *Gyógyàszat*, which features most of the Ferenczian output before 1908.

1894

Sándor Ferenczi obtains his medical diploma, then leaves to complete a year's military service as a doctor in the Austro-Hungarian army. After this, he returns to Budapest, where he starts in general practice.

1897

He is appointed as an intern at the Rókus Hospital in Budapest, which specializes in neurology and neuropathology. He develops his skills in hypnotism and auto-suggestion here.

1898

On 24 July, he is appointed as assistant doctor at the Elizabeth Hospice in Budapest for the poor and prostitutes.

1899

He publishes a long article on telepathy and spiritism ('*Spiritismus*') in *Gyógyàszat*. He follows the ideas of Pierre Janet and Charles Richet, and establishes links between hysterical phenomena, thought transference and prediction. These remain important themes throughout his life's work.

He also writes some fifty articles on the physical condition of the 'disadvantaged', largely based on his work with prostitutes. His call for better treatment, and indeed healthier social conditions, reveals his liberal-socialist political commitment.

1900

He is upgraded to work exclusively as a neurologist at the Elizabeth Hospice, and also sets himself up in private practice in this specialism. He attempts a 'new explanation' of menstruation in *Gyógyàszat* ('A menstruatio magyarázatának ujabb kiserlete'). This prefigures some of his later concerns for primal fluids developed in 'bioanalysis'. He is sent a copy of Freud's *Interpretation of Dreams* to review for *Gyógyàszat*, but decides it is 'not worth the effort' to comment. Later, he regrets this deeply, and inscribes in the front of his copy *'aere perrenius'*, which means 'more solid than bronze'.

1901

He publishes in *Gyógyàszat*, 'Love and science', in which he argues that love resembles a hypnotic state precariously balanced between the normal and the pathological. He soon adds personal experience to this theory.

1902

He publishes 'Female homosexuality' ('*Homosexualitas femina*') in *Gyógyàszat*. This discusses the case of Miss Rósa K., a lesbian transvestite, who was regularly arrested in Vienna and Budapest for soliciting young women while 'disguised' as a man and was finally committed to psychiatric hospital. Ferenczi's sympathetic discussion of her case and his general argument that homosexuality is 'not a disease but a psychic disposition' are instrumental in gaining her release from psychiatric hospital. The Budapest police also issue her an official warrant allowing her to walk in the streets wearing men's clothing. Ferenczi's paper introduces themes he later develops psychoanalytically at the Weimar Congress (1911).

1904

He becomes Head of the Neurology Department and publishes an important study 'On the therapeutic value of hypnotism' ('*A hipnózis gyógyito értekéröl*'). Around this time, he
begins his illicit affair with Gizella Altschul-Pálos.

1905

Dr Magnus Hirschfeld, the prominent Berlin sexologist,
creates an International Humanitarian Committee for the
Defence of Homosexuals, based on the German Society he
had founded in 1897. The main aim is to change criminal law
which universally imposes severe punishments on homosexuals. Ferenczi becomes the Budapest representative of this
organization, signs petitions calling for legal reform and
publishes an article 'On the intermediate sex' ('*Sexualis
átmeneti fokozatokról*', *Gyógyàszat*, 1906) which attacks the
view proposed by eminent medics like Krafft-Ebing and
Möbius that homosexuality is a degenerate disease. In contrast, Freud expresses his sympathy for the committee, but
refuses to be associated with the call for legal reform (cf.
Freud to Jung, 25 February 1908, in Freud and Jung, 1974,
125–6).

1906

C. G. Jung publishes details of his word-association test
(*Diagnostische Assoziationsstudien*, Leipzig, Barth, 1906).
Ferenczi immediately becomes a convert, buys a chronome-
ter and applies the test to anyone who is willing, even custo-

mers in Budapest cafés. On 27 May, at the Congress of South-West German Neurologists and Psychiatrists in Baden-Baden, Jung defends Freud's 'Fragment of an analysis of a case of hysteria' (Freud, 1905e, 7, pp. 3ff.) against a virulent attack from Aschaffenburg and goes on to link his own word-association test to Freudian psychoanalysis ('Psychoanalysis and association experiments', 1906, 2, pp. 288ff.). Jung also sends a copy of the new book to Freud, who opens their copious correspondence with a 'thank you' letter on 11 April. Ferenczi becomes aware of these developments in early 1907, when he writes to Jung in Zürich, suggesting collaboration. At this time, though, both Ferenczi and Jung are still strongly influenced by Pierre Janet's ideas (cf. Jung's *Über die Psychologie der Dementia Praecox* [1907] 1909, 3, pp. 3ff., which combines Freudian and Janetian terminology). In this context, it should be remembered that Jung spent the winter of 1902/3 studying with Janet in Paris and Ferenczi translated Janet's colleague and friend George Dumas into Hungarian.

1907

Jung visits Freud in Vienna on Sunday, 3 March, and attends the Wednesday evening meeting of Freud's circle on 6 March. The following week, Jung proceeds to Budapest and stays with Dr Fülop Stein (1867–1918), a friend and colleague of Ferenczi. Jung and Ferenczi meet and engage in lengthy discussions during this visit. On 28 June, Jung writes to Freud that 'Dr Stein of Budapest and another mental specialist, Dr Ferenczi, want to visit you some time in Vienna and have asked me to enquire when it would be most convenient for you' (Freud and Jung, 1974, pp. 65–6).

1908

Stein and Ferenczi visit Freud on Sunday, 2 February. Ferenczi and Freud get on so well that Freud invites him to give a paper at the first psychoanalytical congress in Salzburg and to join the Freud family on holiday in Berchtesgaden in August. On the evening of 27 April, in the Hotel Bristol in Salzburg, Ferenczi presents a paper on 'What practical hints for child education can be drawn from Freudian experience?'. In May, Jung receives Otto Gross in Zürich for treatment for cocaine and opium addiction. Gross is generally considered to be a rising star in the psychoanalytic firmament. Freud states that only Gross and Jung are capable of making an 'original contribution' to psychoanalysis (25 February 1908, Freud and Jung, 1974, p. 126); Ernest Jones claims that Gross is 'the nearest approach to the romantic ideal of a genius I have ever met' (1959, p. 173). Gross's book *Über Psychopathische Minderwertigkeiten* ('On Psychopathic Inferiorities') is greeted as one of the intellectual highlights of the year: 'another outstanding work', writes Freud, 'full of bold syntheses and overflowing with ideas' (3 June 1908, Freud and Jung, 1974, p. 227). From the outset, the Gross/ Jung exchange develops way beyond a simple treatment for drug dependency. They soon move on to the state of the psychoanalytic art, and Jung takes on board many of Gross's ideas on sexual freedom. The sessions also take on some of the relaxed characteristics of Gross's psychoanalytic technique, which was elaborated, according to Jones, around cross-table repartee at the Café Passage in Munich, chosen especially because it was open twenty-four hours a day. 'Whenever I got stuck, he analysed me', Jung writes to Freud on 25 May (p. 153). Gross soon tires of the drug prohibition and writes 'Dear Jung, I climbed over the asylum wall and am now in the Hotel X. This is a begging letter. Please send me money for the hotel expenses and also the train fare to Munich' (Jones, 1959, p. 174). In any case, this analysis serves as a model for 'mutual analysis', later evolved by Ferenczi.

1909

On 7 February, Freud's eldest daughter Mathilde marries Robert Hollitscher. Freud writes to Ferenczi on the same day, thanking him for his wedding congratulations and confessing that he wished Ferenczi had been the lucky man.

On 10 June, Sabina Spielrein writes to Freud informing him of her love affair with Jung. Spielrein, a twenty-four-year-old medical student, was previously Jung's patient and clearly feels cruelly abused. Freud seriously doubts his choice of 'crown prince', especially as Spielrein suggests there may be ideological motives. 'Jung arrives', she informs Freud, 'beaming with pleasure, and tells me with strong emotion about Gross, about the great insight he has received [about polygamy] and he no longer wants to suppress his feeling for me' (Carotenuto, 1982, p. 107). Jung confesses to Freud: 'Gross and Spielrein are bitter experiences. To none of my patients have I extended so much friendship and from none have I reaped so much sorrow' (4 June 1908, Freud and Jung, 1974, p. 229). The next time Freud and Jung meet is on 20 August in the company of Ferenczi at Bremen. During dinner, Freud and Ferenczi convince Jung to abandon his strict temperance and agree that alcohol may even in some circumstances be quite pleasant. Freud laughs so much that he faints. Following their free-associative bent, the three liberally interpret the incident. Freud stresses his deep suspicions of Jung in the wake of the Gross/Spielrein affairs; Jung

intimates unresolved homoerotic tension in Freud; and Ferenczi struggles with some prophetic sense of deep shifts in
psychoanalytic concerns, notably towards the occult. When a
similar incident occurs in Munich in November 1912, Ferenczi feels the two events are prophetically linked in a chain
of 'deferred actions' (letter to Freud, 28 November 1912 – see
p. 58 for an explanation of the source of the Freud/Ferenczi
correspondence).

On 21 August, the three set sail in the *George Washington*
and arrive in New York in the evening of Sunday, 29 August.
After a week's sight-seeing, they arrive at Clark University,
Worcester, Massachusetts, on Sunday, 5 September. For the
next five days, Freud lectures every morning at 11 a.m.,
following a walk and discussion with Ferenczi, Jung gives
three lectures on his word-association experiments and dementia praecox. Although both Freud and Jung lecture in
German, it is likely that the American audience is more
familiar with Jung's work, as Adolf Meyer has recently published on his experiments with the association test in the New
York Psychiatric Institute. In any case, it is certain that Janet
has a far greater following than either of them, after his
lectures at the Lowell Institute in Boston in 1904 and his 1906
lectures at Harvard (published in English as *The Major
Symptoms of Hysteria*, Macmillan, 1907). This surely explains why Freud dedicates most of his second lecture to a
criticism of Janet. On Saturday, 11 September, both Freud
and Jung receive honorary doctorates of law from Clark
University. The three then spend the next two days travelling
to Niagara Falls. They return to New York after a brief visit
to James Jackson Putnam's family camp near Lake Placid.
On Tuesday, 21 September, they board the *Kaiser Wilhelm
der Grosse* and set sail for Bremen, arriving on the 29th. Jung
heads straight off home to Küssnacht, but Freud and Fe-

renczi visit Hamburg and Berlin. On 1 October, in Berlin, they both visit a medium called Frau Seidler, who illustrates her telepathic powers by reading written scripts while blind-folded. On their return to their respective homes, Freud and Ferenczi correspond at length about this aspect of 'thought transference' (*Übertragung*) (cf. Freud to Ferenczi, 6 October). This theme figures prominently in Ferenczi's 'Introjection and transference', which appears in the *Jahrbuch der Psychoanalyse* (1909).

1910

In the early evening of 30 March, Ferenczi concludes the opening session of the Second Psychoanalytical Congress at Nuremberg with a report 'On the need for closer alliance among adherents of Freud's teachings, with suggestions for a permanent international organization'. He proposes the creation of the International Psycho-Analytical Association (IPA). 'The psycho-analytically trained', he argues, 'are surely the best adapted to found an association which would combine the greatest possible personal liberty with the advantages of family organization. It would be a family in which the father enjoyed no dogmatic authority, but only that to which he was entitled by reason of his abilities and labours' (3, p. 303). Ironically, Ferenczi's report generates such acrimony that discussion has to be abandoned and rescheduled for the following morning. Alfred Adler and Wilhelm Stekel interpret deep anti-Viennese sentiment in Ferenczi's presentation, particularly his suggestion that Jung and the Zürich school are more 'scientific', hence better qualified to lead the IPA. They organize an impromptu protest meeting in Stekel's room in the Grand Hotel, which

Freud gate-crashes to utter 'My enemies would be willing to see me starve; they would tear my very coat off my back'. As befits the Ferenczian idea of the 'non-dogmatic' father, Freud later proposes a compromise that effectively removes himself from the formal (though unreal) position of front-runner. He resigns his position as President of the Vienna Psycho-Analytical Society to make way for Adler. To counterbalance Jung's editorship of the *Jahrbuch für Psychoanalyse*, a new monthly *Zentralblatt für Psychoanalyse* is proposed that will be edited jointly by Adler and Stekel. Following this, the tension subsides and the IPA is formally approved, with Jung elected as President. Jung appoints his Zürich colleague Franz Riklin as Secretary, a bizarre choice since Riklin is pathologically inefficient, and little if any administration takes place. On 3 April, Freud writes to Ferenczi that 'I believe that my long-pent-up aversion for the Viennese combined with your brother complex to make us short-sighted' (Jones, 2, p. 78). Soon this self-referential distance collapses again into open reproach. 'The tactlessness and unpleasant behaviour of Adler and Stekel make it very difficult to get along together. I am chronically exasperated with both of them. Jung also, now that he is President, might put aside his sensitiveness about earlier incidents' (letter to Ferenczi, 8 November). In August, Freud meets Gustav Mahler in Leyden, in the Netherlands, for lunch and a four-hour 'brief analysis', where they mutually explore the aetiology of the composer's neurosis. Afterwards, Ferenczi joins Freud on a holiday journey incorporating Paris, Florence, Rome, Naples, Palermo and Syracusa. Ferenczi's literary production mirrors the general climate in the IPA. His essay 'On obscene words' draws attention to unconscious infantile aggression operating within everyday language. Curiously, the essay is featured in the first number of Adler and Stekel's *Zentralblatt*.

1911

Adler gives two papers at the Vienna Psycho-Analytical Society, on 4 January and 1 February which raise considerable dissent. Some members even suggest that Adlerian views are incompatible with psychoanalysis. Given the clear lack of consensus, at the committee meeting of 22 February Adler and Stekel propose to resign their respective positions of President and Vice-President. At this point, everyone else resigns, and an emergency meeting is called on 1 March. At this, Freud reluctantly agrees to resume his position as President, and a motion is passed to encourage Adler and Stekel to remain within the Society and to thank them for their work. Freud then suggests to Adler that he resign as editor of the *Zentralblatt*, which provokes him to resign from the Society altogether. He attends his last meeting on 24 May, and then creates a 'Society for Free Psychoanalysis', which is joined by most of Adler's sympathizers. Stekel is an exception, remaining 'on good terms' with and 'consistently loyal' to Freud (letter from Freud to Ferenczi, 5 July 1911). In July, Elma Pálos, Gizella's twenty-four-year-old elder daughter, becomes so seriously depressed after the suicide of her lover that she decides to consult Ferenczi. Ferenczi falls passionately in love with her and announces to Freud 'an almost certain engagement'. The 'analysis' quickly runs out of control. Ferenczi feels himself to be a 'football' between mother and daughter (letter to Freud, 12 April 1913) and asks Freud to intervene. Elma feels she is 'immature, spiteful, vain, and love-starved' (letter from Elma Laurvick to Michael Balint, 7 May 1966) and agrees to start analysis with Freud in Vienna in November. In August, Ferenczi joins Freud on holiday in the Dolomites and much time is spent discussing sexual problems. Much of this carries over into Ferenczi's paper 'On the nosology of male homosexuality', which he delivers at the Weimar Congress on the morning of 21 September (1, pp. 296–318). In this, he attempts to construct an 'object relations' theory which can explain the coexistence and sometimes fusion (*amphimixis*) of sexualities.

1912

In April, Elma decides to finish with Freud, return to Budapest, and continue analysis with Ferenczi. This creates impossible tensions and Elma decides to leave for the United States, much to the distress of Ferenczi. He joins Freud for an Easter vacation on the Dalmatian (now Yugoslavian) island of Rab. On Ferenczi's return to Budapest, it is likely that he sees Melanie Klein for the first time. She is thirty years old, nine years unhappily married, mother of two (soon three) and in need of 'the best nerve specialist in Budapest'. She remains in analysis with Ferenczi periodically until 1919.

On 25 May, Freud leaves for Kreuzlingen, Switzerland, for a weekend visit to Ludwig Binswanger, friend and founder of existential psychoanalysis, who is seriously ill. Freud also expects to see Jung on this visit, as Kreuzlingen is not far from Zürich, but Jung claims the letter arrived after Freud had returned to Vienna. Both interpret this incident as illustrative of the other's unconscious aggression and their relations grow colder.

On 30 May, Stekel and Tausk mutually insult each other at a meeting of the Vienna Psycho-Analytical Society. Tausk claims that Stekel can neither spell nor construct a sentence properly. Stekel declares that not one line of Tausk's will appear in the *Zentralblatt* (which he edits). Freud deems this attitude totally inappropriate for an editor and asks Stekel to resign from this function. Stekel refuses to cede the editorship, but resigns from the Vienna Society. Freud writes to the *Zentralblatt*'s publishers, Bergmann, asking them to remove Stekel; they refuse, because previous cash transactions might be prejudiced.

In July, Jones meets Ferenczi in Vienna and they formulate the idea of a 'secret committee' to monitor psychoanalytic developments and prevent future division. They discuss this with Otto Rank and decide to write to Freud, who is in Karlsbad at the time (Ernest Jones to Freud, 30 July). Freud approves the idea and they agree to include themselves, Karl Abraham, Hanns Sachs and Ferenczi's close Budapest friend Anton von Freund.

There is no usual annual congress in September, as Jung has made alternative arrangements. He gives highly publicized lectures at Fordham University, New York, in which he openly criticizes Freud's views. During this month, Freud and Ferenczi take a short vacation together in Rome. On his return, Jung calls an emergency meeting of the IPA to discuss the *Zentralblatt* issue. This convenes (without Ferenczi) at the Park Hotel in Munich at 9 a.m. on 24 November. They agree to leave the *Zentralblatt* to Stekel and found a new journal, the *Internationale Zeitschrift für ärztliche Psychoanalyse*. Freud will be the general editor of this, assisted by Ferenczi, Rank and Jones as executive editors. Over lunch, Jung and Abraham engage in a spirited argument about the Egyptian King Amenhotep IV. Abraham infers that the King's removal of his father's name and inscriptions wherever they occurred implies that patricide underlies the Amenhotepian discovery of monotheism. Jung counters this by suggesting that the removal of fathers' names was commonplace and, even if there were patricidal motives, these are nothing in comparison with the benefits of monotheism. At this point, Freud faints at table. Amid the ensuing commotion, Jung picks him up, carries him through to the next room and lays him on a sofa. Henceforth, Freud's prized statuette of Amenhotep, which sits on his desk, assumes an added significance.

1913

Freud and Jung celebrate the New Year by agreeing to end their personal correspondence, after an acrid exchange of counter-accusations (Freud to Jung, 3 January; Jung to Freud, 6 January, Freud and Jung, 1974). They continue, however, to communicate about IPA business. They both also inform their colleagues of the state of affairs between them. Ferenczi tries to avert the imminent secession of the Zürich Society but is told by Alphonse Maeder that the main difference is between Jews and 'Aryans'. Freud advises Ferenczi to abandon his efforts on 8 May.

Meanwhile Ferenczi takes a three-week Easter holiday in Corfu and Greece with his friend Schächter. He views himself as a 'valet' serving both Gizella and Elma, and suffers from numerous minor ailments (letter to Freud, 12 April). When Elma announces her forthcoming marriage to Laurvick in America, he develops pains around the heart. He returns to Budapest and undergoes a nose operation in April.

On 19 May, the Budapest Psychoanalytical Society is founded. Ferenczi is President, and remains so until his death. Istvan Hollos (1872–1957) becomes Vice-President. Like Ferenczi, Hollos is a prominent psychiatrist in Budapest, who is active in reformist and radical literary groups, and is particularly dedicated to psychoanalytic transformation of psychiatric hospitals (trenchantly encapsulated in his novel *Farewell to the Yellow House*, 1928). Sándor Rado is appointed as Secretary.

Anton von Freund uses some of the wealth gained from the brewing trade to ensure against insolvency and Lajos Levy agrees to deal with the financial details. Ferenczi's friend Hugo Ignotus 'functions as the audience' (Jones, 2, p. 116). Ignotus, an eminent poet, edits the avant-garde journal *Nyugat* ('The West'). From the outside, the Society appears quite subversive, as it contains vociferous and renowned advocates of world communism, gay rights, anti-militarism and the imminent collapse of the Habsburg Empire.

On 25 May, Freud presents a gold ring bearing a Graeco-Roman intaglio to each member of the 'secret committee'. Ferenczi's ring depicts Dionysus, with highly erect penis, and two goddesses looking on admiringly.

In May, Ernest Jones visits Vienna and is advised by Freud to go into analysis with Ferenczi. Jones proceeds to Budapest and sees Ferenczi for an hour twice a day for much of the summer and autumn. This is hailed as the first 'training or didactic analysis'.

On Friday, 8 August, Pierre Janet reads his report on 'psychoanalysis' to the Seventeenth International Congress of Medicine in London. He is reasonably favourable, but claims that Freud borrowed some of his own concepts. Jung, in reply, is even more critical of Freud.

In August, Freud meets Ferenczi's mother, Rósa, in Marienbad. The Freuds and Ferenczi proceed to San Martino di Castrozza in the Dolomites for their summer vacation. They are joined there by Abraham and journey together to Munich for the Fourth IPA Congress. This takes place on 7 and 8 September in the Hotel Bayrischer Hof. Despite conciliatory remarks on all sides, the meetings generate great tension and bad feeling. Twenty-two (of fifty-two voters) abstain in the 'procedural' vote on Jung's re-election as IPA President. Jung accuses Ferenczi in particular of betraying him through his abstention. In reply, Ferenczi claims that no one even remotely conceived of abstaining before Jung acted throughout the congress in a 'one-sided and partial' way (Ferenczi to Jung, 3 November). In fact, Ferenczi's differences from Jung are clearly spelt out in his Congress paper, 'Belief, disbelief, and conviction' (2, pp. 437–50). This criticizes Jung's lack of 'special stress on the patient's re-living over again each individual traumatic infantile experience, and contents itself with a general indication of the archaic character of the symptoms or with a few examples that are to convince the patient of this' (2, p. 449).

Immediately after the Congress, Freud travels to Rome. He is joined at Bologna by his sister-in-law, Minna Bernays, and they spend 'seventeen delicious days there'.

Jung hears from Maeder that Freud doubts his bona fides, so writes to Freud on 27 October that 'since this is the gravest reproach that can be levelled at anybody, you have made further collaboration impossible' (p. 550). Jung resigns his editorship of the *Jahrbuch*, but keeps the Presidency of the IPA.

On 30 October, the London Psychoanalytical Society is founded. Jones is President, Douglas Bryen Vice-President and David Eder Secretary.

1914

In the first volume of the new *Zeitschrift*, Ferenczi publishes an extensive criticism of Jung's *Psychology of the Unconscious* ('*Kritik der Jungschen* Wandlungen und Symbole der Libido', i, pp. 391–403; cf. Freud's letter to Jung, 29 November 1912, Freud and Jung, 1974, p. 524). On 20 April, Jung writes to Freud to tender his resignation as President of the IPA because his views 'are in such contrast to the views of the majority of the members of our Association' (p. 551). On 30 April, Freud addresses a circular letter to all heads of the European societies to explain the situation and propose the temporary election of Karl Abraham as President of the IPA. He suggests that Abraham's location in Berlin ideally suits his role as organizer of the Fifth Congress in Dresden in September. In fact, this Congress never takes place. The Fifth Congress will be organized by Ferenczi and take place in Budapest on 28/29 September 1918.

On 28 April, the Archduke Franz Ferdinand of Austria is assassinated in Sarajevo, Serbia, thus precipitating an international crisis between the Habsburg Empire and Russia over control of the Balkans. Germany agrees to support the Habsburg position, and the Russians, Austro-Hungarians and Germans all mobilize their armies. In July, Europe collapses into war.

On 30 September, Ferenczi begins an analysis with Freud in Vienna. This lasts three weeks, as it is interrupted by the mobilization. Ferenczi is conscripted and posted for two years, as a doctor in the Hungarian Hussars, to Pápá, a small garrison about eighty miles from Budapest. Besides the interruption of his analysis and the intractable emotional difficulty with Gizella and Elma, his main problem is with boredom. The town is well supplied with provisions and he is able to send the Freud family food parcels and precious Trabuko cigars in beleaguered Vienna. He is even able to visit Freud for the odd few days of leave. On the whole, though, the Freud/Ferenczi correspondence has to take over the frustration of the truncated analysis.

1915

The war breaks into Ferenczi's inner world when the first shell-shock victims arrive. He is particularly taken with what he calls 'the first psychoanalysis on horseback' which he undertakes while riding with his company commander (Ferenczi to Freud, 22 February). He spends the year in Pápá, except for the occasional week's leave. In his leisure time, he translates Freud's *Three Essays on the Theory of Sexuality* (1905d, 7, pp. 125ff.) into Hungarian, sketches a first draft of *Versuch einer Genitaltheorie* (*Thalassa*) and writes up many of his earlier case-notes and project articles.

1916

In the spring, Jones writes to Freud that he has eleven patients and three on the waiting-list; moreover, he has bought a car and a house in the country. Freud relays the news to Ferenczi, who replies 'Oh happy England! . . . well, it doesn't look like there is going to be an early end to the war!' (Ferenczi to Freud, 22 July; cf. Jones, 2, p. 211).

At about the same time, Ferenczi is transferred back to Budapest as director of a neurological clinic whose main task is to treat shell-shock victims. He writes up his preliminary views on the psychoanalytic treatment of war neuroses, which are published the following year ('*Über zwei Typen der Kriegsneurose*', *Zeitschrift*, iv, pp. 131–45). In mid-June, he is granted three weeks' leave to visit Freud and takes up his analysis again during this period for two hours a day. He is surprised to learn that Freud has not other patients at this time and little prospect of new ones within the foreseeable future (cf. Freud to Ferenczi, 22 December).

1917

In February, Ferenczi suffers from a mysterious illness, which is attributed to a range of causes from tuberculosis to 'exophthalmic goitre' and 'Basedow's disease with psychological components' (cf. Ferenczi to Freud, 21 February; Sabourin, 1985, p. 109; Jones, 2, p. 217). His sister Zsófia claims he suffered internal bleeding after swallowing something (Dupont, 1988, p. 36). In any case, he is sent for convalescence to Semmering, Austria, for three months. For much of this time he meditates on his personal predicament and decides to propose to Gizella. He is afraid of her reply, so asks her to convey her decision to Freud. Freud, on the contrary, requests her to reply directly to Ferenczi (cf. exchange of letters of 24 and 25 March). She is still unsure, but starts to prepare her husband Géza for divorce.

During the summer, some members of the 'secret committee', Ferenczi, Freud, Rank, Sachs, and Eitingon, manage to meet for a few weeks on Csorbató, in the Tatra Mountains in (Czecho)Slovakia. The Budapest and Vienna Societies also arrange a joint meeting in Vienna, where Melanie Klein meets Freud for the first time (Klein, *Autobiography*, manuscript, Klein Trust).

Freud's *Introductory Lectures* (1915–16, 16–17) appear in the autumn. Freud and Ferenczi start work on a joint study of the influence of Lamarckism on psychoanalysis, which they define as follows: 'Our intention is to place Lamarck entirely on our basis and to show that his "need" which creates and transforms organs is nothing other than the power of unconscious ideas over the body, of which we see relics in hysteria; in short, the "omnipotence of thoughts"' (Jones, 2, p. 219). At the same time, Ferenczi mourns the death of his friend Schächter.

1918

Dr Anton von Freund has a cancerous growth on his testicle removed and consults Freud afterwards for post-operative depression. Freund decides to donate some of his fortune to create a psychoanalytic publishing house, the Internationaler Psychoanalytischer Verlag, but there are problems transferring the money from Budapest to Vienna and, later, with Austrian government approval. Otto Rank moves temporarily to Budapest to help with the preliminary administration and his friendship with Ferenczi deepens.

Ferenczi secures the same holiday accommodation in Csorbató as last year. On 5 July, Anna and Sigmund Freud take a Danube steamer to Steinbruch in Hungary, where they stay for a couple of days with some of von Freund's relatives. They then proceed to Csorbató, where they meet Ferenczi.

On 28 and 29 September, the Fifth IPA Congress is held in the hall of the Hungarian Academy of Sciences in Budapest. Austrian, German and Hungarian government officials attend to be fully informed of psychoanalytic work with war neuroses and plan to establish psychoanalytic treatment centres for these disorders. The first is to be in Budapest (Ferenczi to Freud, 8 October). The mayor and city council of Budapest hold a reception for the participants, reserving the new luxury Hotel Gellért-Fürdö for them. Freud claims that Budapest has become the 'centre of the psychoanalytical movement' (cf. letter to Abraham, 27 August). The main theme of the Congress is the development of psychoanalytic technique. Freud reads a paper on 'Lines of advance in psychoanalytic therapy'; Ferenczi complements this with a paper on 'Technical difficulties in the analysis of a case of hysteria' (2, pp. 189ff.). For the first time, Ferenczi mentions 'active' technique, focusing on the hypnotic 'suggestion' model. At the end of the Congress, Ferenczi is elected President of the IPA.

The armistice is signed in Padua, Italy, on 3 November. The liberal Count Mihály Károlyi proclaims Hungary a Republic on 16 November. At the same time, the Czechs advance into Slovakia, or 'Upper Hungary' as it is then called. The Rumanians and Serbs declare their independence and occupy Hungarian territory that they consider their own. Oszkar Jászi, the new Minister of Nationalities, attempts to create an 'Eastern Switzerland' by negotiation with the Czechs, Rumanians and Serbs, but fails miserably. Similarly, Károlyi's new electoral reform is considered too radical by the Right, and Count Batthyáni, the Interior Minister, resigns. By the end of November, then, the country is politically divided, militarily occupied and suffering from chronic food shortages.

In this context, the Hungarian Communist Party is formed in Budapest on 24 November. Its leader is Béla Kun, an activist in the Russian Revolution and friend of Lenin. Kun's policy involves diplomatic alliance with the Soviet Union, rather than the West, and extensive social reform, including rapid educational expansion and a national health service. Senior members of the Budapest Psychoanalytical Society are influential in this, notably Hugo Ignotus, Sándor Rado, Imre Hermann and Ferenczi.

1919

Between 1 and 5 January, Budapest factories are occupied and the government sends in troops. On 11 January, Károlyi becomes President of a new government which includes five socialists (from the Hungarian Social Democratic Party). This does not calm discontent. On 21 February, the Communist Party leaders are arrested, and this also fails to restore order. On 26 February, the Paris Peace Conference decides to create a neutral zone in south-east Hungary to separate Hungarian and Rumanian forces. This effectively convinces many Hungarians of Kun's assertion that more is to be gained from alliance with the Soviet Union than from the West's Peace Conference. The socialists (SDP) shift to support him, and Károlyi resigns. The new 'Revolutionary Governing Council' is proclaimed on 22 March.

On 1 March, Ferenczi marries Gizella. On their arrival at the town hall, they are told that her ex-husband, Géza Pálos, has just died of a heart attack.

On 29 March, all schools, universities and educational institutes become state property. György Lukács, the People's Commissar for Education, announces a reform of universities. Ferenczi becomes the first Professor of Psychoanalysis, Roheim the first Professor of Anthropology and Revesz the first Professor of Experimental Psychology. Ferenczi's appointment was originally mooted the previous year (letter of Ferenczi to Freud, 25 October 1918): over one thousand students petition the Rector of Budapest University asking that Ferenczi be appointed to give a series of lectures on psychoanalysis; Hugo Ignotus gains the Károlyi government's approval for this; but it is only under Lukács' authority that the appointment actually takes place.

On 16 April, the Hungarian Red Army fails to contain the Rumanian advance and surrenders all territories east of the River Tisza. The socialists call an emergency meeting and resign from the 'Revolutionary Governing Council' on 2 May. Kun refuses to resign and doubles the size of the Red Army, which starts to have some success in early June. At this time, Rear-Admiral Miklós Horthy de Nagybánya, former Commander-in-Chief of the Austro-Hungarian Navy, creates a rival 'National Army' in Szeged, a garrison town in French-occupied territory. The Rumanians counter-attack the Red Army, and by 31 July are 100 kilometres from Budapest. On 1 August, Kun and the Council resign, after only 133 days in office.

Meanwhile, in Vienna, in the early hours of 3 July, Viktor Tausk sips slivovitz, writes letters to his wife and Freud, then blows his head off. Freud informs the 'committee' the following day.

On 3 August, Rumanian troops march unopposed into Budapest. Numerous attempts to form governments are overturned by armed insurrection. Horthy's troops advance into areas not occupied by the Rumanians and ruthlessly persecute 'radicals' and Jews. This 'white terror' rages until the autumn, by which time some 5,000 are killed and 70,000 imprisoned. The Paris Peace Conference representatives do nothing to stop this when they arrive in Budapest on 5 August. On 16 November, Horthy enters Budapest at the head of the National Army.

On 27 September, a reduced 'committee' of Freud, Ferenczi, Jones and Rank meet in Vienna. Jones is shocked by the city, whose hardship seems summarized by 'the vain efforts of the emaciated dogs to stagger to the food I throw them' (3, p. 17). Ferenczi remarks that conditions are even worse in Budapest. They all decide that it is prudent for Ferenczi to resign as President of the IPA, and that Jones assume this function forthwith.

1920

On 20 January, Anton von Freund dies of cancer. Five days later, Freud's daughter Sophie dies of pneumonia. Freud writes to Ferenczi: 'Quite deep down I can trace the feeling of a deep narcissistic wound that is not to be healed' (4 February).

On 14 February, the Berlin Psychoanalytic Polyclinic is launched, with ambitious plans for a training programme and free psychoanalytic treatment for the poor. Sachs and Theodor Reik move there to assist with the work.

Freud is appointed by the Austrian military authorities to report to a special commission established to investigate complaints of cruel treatment of shell-shock victims in the Psychiatric Division of the Vienna General Hospital. Freud's report, dated 23 February, claims that electrical shock treatment is inappropriate for war neuroses. Julius Wagner-Jauregg, the Director of the Psychiatric Division, never forgives him for this. A collective work, *Zur Psychoanalyse der Kriegsneurosen* ([1919] 1921), written by Freud, Ferenczi, Abraham, Simmel and Jones, causes considerable stir in medical circles in March.

On 1 March, Horthy is declared 'Regent' of Hungary and introduces a series of reactionary laws, including the re-introduction of corporal punishment in schools and the severe restriction of university entrance. The Communist Party is banned and Jews are effectively removed or barred from a range of professions. Ferenczi's university position is closed and he is dismissed from the Hungarian Medical Association. Furthermore, the Mayor of Budapest demands an official enquiry into the 'status' of psychoanalysis and confiscates some of the Budapest Society's funds. The enquiry is condemnatory, leaving Ferenczi desolate and sorely tempted to go into exile. Freud advises a tougher approach with the 'cowardly and deceitful animals' (letter to Ferenczi, 1 January).

From 30 March to 9 April, the 'committee' meets in Vienna, with the exception of Abraham and Eitingon, who cannot acquire papers to travel from Berlin.

The sixth IPA Congress is held between 8 and 12 September in the 'Pulchri Studio' in the Society of Artists, in The Hague, Holland. Ferenczi presents his paper on 'Further development of the active technique in Psychoanalysis' (2, pp. 198ff.). He also meets Georg Groddeck, who presents a paper on 'The psychoanalysis of the organic'. Finally, Ferenczi introduces Melanie Klein to Karl Abraham, and the latter invites her to Berlin to pursue her interests in child analysis.

1921

Rósa Ferenczi dies.

On 17 August, Ferenczi writes to Groddeck asking if Gizella and he may book rooms for the following month in Groddeck's Sanatorium – or Satanarium, as his patients call it – in Baden-Baden, Germany. They arrive on 5 September, and the Ferenczis and Groddecks soon become close friends. Ferenczi discusses the disappointments of his relationship with Freud in correspondence with Groddeck (see especially the letter from Ferenczi of Christmas Day, pp. 55ff.).

On 20 September, all the 'committee' rendez-vous in Berlin and set off on a ten-day working holiday in the Harz Mountains. They go for long walks, and most end up with heavy colds. Freud reads them his paper 'Psychoanalysis and telepathy', which is rapturously received by Ferenczi and cold-shouldered by Jones (Freud, 1922a, 18, pp. 197ff.). Ferenczi presents his view that nervous tics are the product of frustrated masturbation compulsion (2, pp. 142ff.; 3, pp. 349ff.).

1922

During the first week in January, Abraham, Ferenczi, Roheim and Sachs give guest lectures for foreign students of psychoanalysis in Vienna. One of the students, Horace Frink, causes a scandal when he returns to New York in June and proposes to marry a patient. Freud is called in to intervene and advise both parties, who have to negotiate difficult divorces and social uproar. The affair considerably distresses Freud, and reinforces his hostility to any 'mutualism' in analysis. Frink later dies in a state of manic excitement in a psychiatric hospital in 1935.

On 22 May, the Vienna Psychoanalytic Polyclinic or 'Ambulatorium' opens. Eduard Hitschmann is its Director. Like the one in Berlin, the clinic aims to offer free treatment and an intensive psychoanalytic training programme.

Ferenczi and Rank spend August together on vacation in Seefeld. Sachs and Abraham visit them there and they agree to recommend that 'committee' members henceforth address each other as '*Du*' (thou) rather than the more formal '*Sie*' (you). A full assembly of the 'committee' meets on Saturday, 23 September, in Berlin, two days before the Congress.

The Seventh IPA congress takes place in Berlin from 25 to 27 September. This is the last Congress Freud attends. Melanie Klein and Karen Horney present their first papers here. Ferenczi tries out psychoanalytical theories of sexual development that later grow into *Thalassa* ('*Versuch einer Genitaltheorie*').

1923

In February, Freud notices a growth on the inside of his right jaw and palate, and he has it removed on 20 April. Unfortunately, it recurs and is discovered to be malignant. He has the whole right-side upper jaw and palate removed in a two-part operation on 4 and 11 October. For the following sixteen years he has to wear a huge prosthesis, which gives him great discomfort and makes talking difficult. On 7 November, he undergoes a vasectomy (Steinach operation) in the erroneous hope that this will rejuvenate him and ward off the return of cancer.

On 23 April, Freud launches a new 'structural' model of the psyche in *The Ego and the Id* (1923b, 19, pp. 3ff.). This develops and adds to his 'discovery' of the death-drive in *Beyond the Pleasure Principle* (1920g, 18, pp. 3ff.).

On 7 July, Ferenczi celebrates his fiftieth birthday. A special number of the *Zeitschrift* is released for the occasion. It is crowned by an appreciation by Freud, which both surveys Ferenczi's work and offers a succinct portrait of the relevant neuroses: 'Ferenczi occupies a central position in our large community. His struggle in analysis against a strong "brother-complex" has transformed him into an irreproachable elder brother, an excellent teacher, and promoter of young talent'.

On 26 August, the 'committee' meets at Castel Toblino. The conversations are tense, partly because of concern about Freud's health and partly because of growing differences of opinion about psychoanalytic technique. Ferenczi's 'active' method is particularly hotly disputed by Abraham. Ferenczi, in rebuttal, accuses the Berlin Society of being too theoretical at the expense of their clinical performance. Rank later suggests the 'committee' should dissolve itself.

1924

This year opens with continued controversy over proposed revisions in psychoanalytic technique. Ferenczi publishes a defence of 'inhibiting or directing' the patient's free association in a paper in the *Zeitschrift* ('On forced fantasies – activity in the association technique', pp. 68ff.). The controversy is further fuelled by the publication of *The Development of Psychoanalysis* ('*Entwicklungszwiele der Psychoanalyse*'), which Ferenczi co-authors with Rank. Among other things, they argue here for the shortening of analysis and the clear setting of time-limits, to pressure the patient to abandon the last 'resistance', that is, the desire to prolong analysis indefinitely. At this time, ironically, Ferenczi begins his analysis of Elizabeth Severn, which lasts eight years. Initially, Freud is extremely positive about the book. 'Its discovery is magnificent,' he writes to Ferenczi (1 June). He becomes rapidly disenchanted when Rank publishes *The Trauma of Birth* ('*Das Trauma der Geburt*') a month later. In this, Rank suggests that all childhood traumas are just 'screen memories' for 'the most painful memory of all, the trauma of birth' (Rank, 1929, p. 8). For Freud, and indeed Ferenczi, this displays criminal neglect of real child abuse and its oedipal configuration.

Ferenczi is clearly concerned to distance himself from the birth trauma thesis. To some extent, this is achieved by the publication of *Thalassa* later in the year, in which Ferenczi proposes a much more subtle developmental model revolving around five 'catastrophes' (rather than a single 'trauma'): the division of chromosomes into male and female, production of sperm and ova, the unification of sperm and ovum in the womb, birth, then puberty. None the less, the 'courage' of this project (as Freud puts it) is seen to cast more light on biology than on psychoanalysis (Freud, 'Sándor Ferenczi', 1924). The confusions surrounding 'active analysis' have to be clarified elsewhere.

The first occasion for group discussion on this is the Eighth IPA Congress, which meets at Salzburg from 21 to 23 April. Ferenczi's defence of his position is complemented by innovatory papers on technique by Melanie Klein and Wilhelm Reich. Melanie Klein, now settled in Berlin and in analysis with Abraham, questions the psychoanalytic model of infant development and proposes 'play technique' as the appropriate medium of child analysis ('The technique of early analysis', 1932, pp. 16ff.). Wilhelm Reich, recently appointed Director of the 'Psychoanalytic Technique' Seminar at the Viennese Ambulatorium, argues for Ferenczian 'active methods' to analyse resistance, which he sees as the main therapeutic objective (Reich, 1925 [1974]). Reich also follows Ferenczi's 'masterly insight' into the importance of masturbation in determining the aetiology of the neuroses (cf. Reich, '*Über Spezifität der Onanieformen*', *Zeitschrift*, 8, 1922).

In the autumn, it becomes clear that Freud can no longer continue as President of the Vienna Psycho-Analytical Society. Following the 'birth trauma' thesis he is loath to appoint Rank, as he had previously intended. Furthermore, Rank has been absent in the United States since the Congress and eventually decides to set up practice in New York. Freud therefore asks Ferenczi to move to Vienna and take over the Presidency and the Directorship of the Ambulatorium. A benefactor, Frau Kraus, offers to build a new clinic with suitable quarters for the new director and his wife. Ferenczi is keen to leave Budapest, but undecided between New York, Berlin or Vienna. Freud is against 'the barbarous dollar' claiming Ferenczi's talent and deeply disappointed when Frau Kraus withdraws her previous offer (Freud to Ferenczi, 12 October; also 18 September 1926, 8 August 1927). Ferenczi decides to stay in Budapest.

1925

On 6 May, Ferenczi and Eitingon join Freud in Vienna for his sixty-ninth birthday.

In early August, Ferenczi visits again, this time to discuss the Bernays Fund to promote analytical training in America and Europe. Ferenczi joins the European steering committee, and a statement is issued to the press (cf. *Time*, 24 July; *New York Times*, 30 July).

The Ninth IPA Congress takes place at Bad Homberg between 2 and 5 September. Ferenczi attempts a balanced criticism of his own 'active' method, and retracts some of the more extreme elements associated with it, such as the imposition of a time-limit ('Contra-indications to the "active" psychoanalytical technique', 2, pp. 217ff.). He also recommends an additional aspect of 'relaxation', in which the analyst should attempt to put patients at ease. One example he cites provokes laughter. It is of a man who suffers from chronic premature ejaculation, whom Ferenczi advises to 'keep the foreskin rolled back behind the corona glandis' to lower the erotic tension (p. 227). Ferenczi comments: 'Unfortunately, I must tell you the remark of a young colleague who came to know of these researches; he said, "Now I know what active technique is, one lets the patient pull his foreskin back"' (p. 228).

The Congress also agrees to set up an 'international training commission'. There is some disagreement, though, about the establishment of general standards and required qualifications, notably on the issue of 'lay', or non-medical, candidates. Ferenczi is a prominent spokesman for lay analysts.

Karl Abraham develops a bad cough in May. He believes it is caused by swallowing a fish bone but, in fact, it is diagnosed later as lung cancer. His condition deteriorates and he dies on Christmas Day.

1926

On 6 May, the 'committee' gather in Freud's *salon* to celebrate his seventieth birthday. They present him with gifts and he announces his retirement from all his duties with the movement. The next day, there is a seven-and-a-half-hour meeting to discuss the future development of psychoanalysis.

In June, the debate on 'lay' analysis rekindles its fervour after Theodor Reik, a non-medical analyst, is sued for 'quackery'. Freud quickly writes *The Question of Lay Analysis* (1926, 20, pp. 179ff.), supporting Reik and the training of non-medical analysts. He calls it a 'bitter' (*scharf*) experience, because he has to argue against some 'ignorant' analysts too (Freud to Ferenczi, 4 July).

In Berlin, the debate develops a special irony. Rado and Klein, both Hungarian exiles and ex-pupils of Ferenczi, assume opposite sides of the fence. Unfortunately, Rado is the more powerful, as he has just assumed editorship of the *Zeitschrift* after Rank's resignation. Melanie Klein's work is mysteriously kept out of the journal. Klein decides to leave for England and settles there permanently in September.

Ferenczi is invited by Frankwood Williams to give a winter series of lectures at the New School for Social Research in New York. Freud and the other members of the 'committee' are against him accepting, mainly because they fear he may settle there. Despite this, Ferenczi accepts and spends a week with Freud in Vienna before proceeding to Cherbourg, to sail on 22 September. Ferenczi begins his lecture series entitled 'Selected Chapters in the Theory and Practice of Psychoanalysis' on 6 October. His weekly lectures last ninety minutes each, and titles include 'Suggestion and psychoanalysis', 'Development of the ego and instincts', 'Freudian metapsychology', 'The technique of psychoanalysis' and 'Character and its possible changes through psychoanalysis'. Ferenczi also continues analysis of some of the American pupils he had seen in Budapest, takes on new patients and gives clinical supervision. He also presents the American Psychoanalytical Association's Christmas lecture on 'Present day problems in psychoanalysis'. In this Ferenczi emphasizes the need to expand postgraduate work in psychoanalysis and to widen research boundaries beyond strictly medical concerns. There is a lively discussion afterwards and a noteworthy exchange of views with Harry Stack Sullivan.

1927

Sándor and Gizella spend free weekends with the de Forests in Connecticut (Izette de Forest, 1954, p. 6). According to some accounts, they are not particularly happy together: Sándor desperately misses Elma and Gizella is proposing to divorce him so that he can one day marry her daughter (letter from Frederic to Vilma Kovács, 8 January 1927; the source of information is Ferenczi and Groddeck, p. 135).

Ferenczi's advocacy of lay analysis causes some controversy among American analysts. Following the Bad Homburg Congress, the New York Legislature, in conference with the American Medical Association, declares lay analysis to be illegal (Ferenczi to Freud, 17 September 1926). Ferenczi finds this preposterous and characteristically creates a Society for Lay Analysts soon after his arrival in New York. This Society applies for IPA recognition, much to Freud's delight, since he considers them a test case, and much to the dismay of Eitingon, the President of the IPA. The latter is more concerned about alienating the majority of American analysts, who may then secede. In May the New York Society reinforces this point by condemning lay analysis outright in a resolution.

The Ferenczis leave New York for London on 3 June. In London, Ferenczi delivers a lecture on 'The adaptation of the family to the child' to the British Psychological Society. It is followed by an interesting exchange of views with Melanie Klein (2, pp. 74ff.). After England, the Ferenczis spend a few days in Paris, then continue to Groddeck's sanatorium in Baden-Baden, where they arrive around 20 June (Ferenczi and Groddeck, p. 108). They spend three weeks of relaxation, massage, hot baths, long walks and fine conversation.

The lay analysis dispute comes to a head at the Tenth IPA Congress at Innsbruck, Austria (2–4 September). A special issue of the *Zeitschrift* dedicated to lay analysis fails to defuse the conflict. A meeting of the 'international training commission' collapses in total disarray, as the Americans in particular do not wish to be forced to accept either lay candidates or lay analysts trained by other IPA groups. Furthermore, the 'committee' becomes deeply divided by the issue. Freud wishes Ferenczi to succeed Eitingon as President of the IPA, but it becomes clear that the election of such a fervent supporter of lay analysis will totally alienate many members. Both Freud and Ferenczi are wary of Jones's election as a 'compromise', since they fear he will organize the acceptance of lay analysis in principle but stifle it in practice (Ferenczi to Freud, 30 June). Finally, Eitingon agrees to continue in office. The solution offered is an administrative one. First, the 'committee' is deemed no longer to be 'secret', but reflects the organizational structure of the IPA – that is, senior officers and 'personalities' are automatically on it. Second, a 'lay analysis' working party is created to look at different IPA groups' procedures and to report on a possible compromise. Henceforth, this committee's reports assume in advance that they will be controversial.

Strangely, for once, Ferenczi's paper on 'The problem of the termination of the analysis' provokes little comment at the Congress (3, pp. 77ff.).

1928

In February, Ferenczi starts his first public lecture series in Budapest since Horthy came to power. He also invites outside speakers for the first time. Wilhelm Reich presents a paper on character analysis in April. Despite this, Ferenczi claims his work is becoming more difficult. He complains about the lack of support and even friendliness of his colleagues. He also writes about a particularly 'complex and worrying case', probably Elizabeth Severn, that takes up much of his time, and obliges him to re-arrange his schedule (letter to Groddeck, 27 July, p. 111).

Ferenczi visits Freud briefly in Vienna in April; Freud finds his prosthesis increasingly painful and requests that his birthday be a quiet occasion this year. Dorothy Burlingham gives him a chow, Lun Yu, which becomes a great comfort and source of pleasure. Ferenczi visits him again on vacation in Semmering in July. Freud leaves with Anna for Berlin on 30 August to have a new prosthesis fitted by a specialist, and Ferenczi travels once more to visit him in the sanatorium in September.

The Ferenczis take a holiday in Spain in October and enjoy the 'atmosphere, colours, people, old buildings . . . and doctors who are half-Breuerians, half-Jungians, without ever having been Freudians' (letter to Groddeck, 17 October, p. 112).

1929

Ferenczi experiences a burst of creativity at the beginning of the year, writes short articles on cases and on the death-drive. Afterwards he suffers from great fatigue and despondency, which are expressed in letters to Freud and Groddeck. In early February, he improves. A day trip to Freud obviously rallies him. 'The Professor is much better', he writes to Groddeck, 'and is experiencing pleasure in working again.' On his own psyche-soma he comments: 'I am just about OK. I am just seeing the end of my major and minor symptoms of various kinds . . . but I am making clear progress in my intuitive understanding of the essence of neuroses' (12 February, Ferenczi and Groddeck, p. 113).

Much of Ferenczi's fatigue, as well as his 'intuitive understanding', derives from a gruelling analytical practice. 'I fear I am swamped by patients', he complains, 'because none want to terminate analysis. There is no question of me taking on others' (letter to Groddeck, 28 October, and Ferenczi/ Groddeck, p. 118).

An added problem is that 'intuitive understanding' of patients leads him to take them on holiday with him. 'I am here at St Moritz (Hotel Schweizerhof) since July', he writes to Groddeck on 16 August, 'and, as usual, I am accompanied by patients and pupils that I don't want to treat in the great heat of Budapest. But the great altitude here does not suit me. I have pains in the heart and find it hard to breathe. . . I wonder if you have somewhere for us (at Baden-Baden) where I can also work. If possible, I would also like to lodge one of my students that you know (Elizabeth Severn), as she is now in a critical phase' (p. 117).

Freud becomes increasingly concerned about the depth of Ferenczi's commitment to his patients, especially about the 'mutual analysis' he sees emerge from it (Ferenczi to Freud, 6 November). Freud's comments obviously hurt Ferenczi, who begins to write less regularly and be more guarded about his work.

At the end of May, the transformed 'committee' meets to discuss strategies for the forthcoming IPA Oxford Congress.

Yet again it is divided over the 'lay analysis' issue, and re-
solves to re-elect Eitingon as President *faute de mieux*. Ferenczi is extremely critical of Jones, as well of the intransi-
gence of the American position. This is hardly surprising,
given that his group of lay analysts in New York was forced
to disband in January.

Ferenczi's paper at the Eleventh IPA Congress in Oxford
in August, 'The principle of relaxation and neocatharsis', is
uncharacteristically guarded and self-referential. He assumes
'awkward objections' and 'general uproar and clamour. . .if
the IPA were not so highly cultivated and dignified' (3,
p. 116). He also expresses his public thanks to Elizabeth
Severn (p. 122).

On 24 October, 'Black Friday', the Wall Street Stock Exchange crashes, initiating a world economic crisis and the
withdrawal of American loans to Europe. Along with the rest
of the world, the IPA, the 'Verlag', the Bernays Fund, the
national psychoanalytic societies and individual analysts are
faced with immediate or imminent bankruptcy.

In November, Elma visits the Ferenczis in Budapest.

1930

In the New Year, Ferenczi and Freud exchange frank letters
about their mutual feelings for each other. On 11 January,
Freud sympathizes with Ferenczi's frustrations concerning lay
analysis, the New York Society and failure to be re-elected
President. He wonders, however, where Ferenczi's hostile feelings towards him originate. On 17 January, Ferenczi replies:

> What happens in the relationship between you and me (at least
> in me) is an entanglement of various conflicts of emotions and

positions. At first you were my revered mentor and unattainable model, for whom I nourished the feelings of a pupil – always somewhat mixed, as we know. Then you became my analyst, but as a result of unfortunate circumstances my analysis could not be completed. I particularly regretted that, in the course of the analysis, you did not perceive in me and did not bring to abreaction negative feelings and fantasies that were only partially transferred.

(p. xiii)

This exchange clears the air. On 21 April, Ferenczi visits Freud for the day and they have a long and fruitful discussion about the direction Ferenczi's work is taking (Ferenczi to Freud, 30 April).

In May, the Ferenczis buy a new villa in Buda, on the other side of town (Lisznyai utca 11 – there is a commemorative plaque on the wall now). Freud writes to Ferenczi, congratulating him on the purchase and reminding him that he had predicted such a move at the Budapest Congress. He regrets, though, that he probably never will be able to visit, but takes prophecy one step further. He predicts that Ferenczi will discover that it is the site of an ancient Roman villa, whose former owner travelled frequently to Egypt and brought back souvenirs, especially statuettes, that would sit perfectly on the desk of an aged analyst in Vienna (Freud to Ferenczi, 28 May). Freud adds wryly: 'My prophetic talent is, like that of all prophets, very one-sided; while we apprehend one element of the future another escapes us'. The Ferenczis move into the villa in July.

Ferenczi's health causes him considerable concern. He writes to Groddeck: 'bad nights one after the other, with headaches and breathing difficulties; after endless attempts, I may have found a way of relief – or at least I am a little better at the moment' (15 June). A month or so later, he writes in a similar vein to Freud, though this time linking the pain to his thought transformations:

> Though somewhat sooner than you, Professor, I too am preoccu-pied with the problem of death. . . Part of my love for the corporeal me appears to have sublimated itself in scientific inter-ests, and this subjective factor has made me sensitive, I think, to the psychic and other processes that take place in neurotics in moments of mortal danger, real or presumed. That was the path which led me to revive the theory of traumatism. (20 July)

On 10 October, Freud has another operation on his jaw. A week later he goes down with bronchial pneumonia and is confined to bed for a fortnight. He is convinced he will die before the year is out and asks Ferenczi to assume the Presi-dency of the IPA in that eventuality. Ferenczi agrees. He writes to Groddeck: 'The trip to Vienna has done me good. The differences of opinion do not have deep roots, on the con-trary. . . we have a clear understanding, in contrast to former discussions. . . as for my projected Presidency, it begins to interest me' (21 December, Ferenczi/Groddeck pp. 121–2).

Throughout this year, Ferenczi dedicates most of his time to his patients.

> I dedicate four sometimes five hours a day to my main patient, 'the Queen' [Elizabeth Severn]. It is tiring but gratifying. I think that soon, or, at least, not too long, I will be able to say what it means to 'end an analysis'. The other patients also 'act out' [*agieren*] spiritedly, and every day confirm what I've written on the need to re-establish the seduction theory. In any case, psy-choanalysis, as I'm now practising it, takes much more out of one than previously has been assumed.
>
> (letter to Groddeck, 21 December, p. 122)

1931

On 11 to 12 May, the Viennese Kreditanstalt Bank collapses, wiping out a large proportion of IPA-related funds. This is followed by the collapse of the Darmstadt and Dresden banks and the closure of all banks in Germany from 12 July to 5 August. The Berlin Society and Polyclinic are declared bankrupt and threatened with imminent closure. Eitingon, their previous benefactor, is ruined, so an appeal is launched among members. Under these circumstances, the IPA Congress planned for Wiesbaden, Germany, in September is postponed.

Despite this, the Budapest Society manages to overcome a government ban and open a polyclinic at Mézaros utca 12, in May. Ferenczi is the director, and Michael Balint his deputy, though, in practice, Ferenczi's contribution is limited by his private practice and health.

In May, Ferenczi sends Freud a first draft of 'Confusion of tongues between adults and the child: the language of tenderness and of passion', the paper he is preparing for the next IPA Congress. Among other things, this proposes a complete revision of Ferenczi's theory of genitality (*Thalassa*) in the light of 'the terrorism of suffering' imposed by sexual attacks. The sexual attack imposes a 'precocious maturity', which Ferenczi theorizes into a separate 'sexual development phase' called 'passion'. The non-abused child object-relates through 'tenderness' and the abused child object-relates through 'passion': 'The perversions, for instance, are perhaps only infantile as far as they remain on the level of tenderness; if they become passionate and laden with guilt, they are perhaps already the result of exogenous stimulation, of secondary, neurotic exaggeration' (3, p. 166). Freud replies critically in June, suggesting that the distinction obscures the function of fantasy in memory and in the progression between phases. He adds that he has never abandoned the view that sexual attacks generate neuroses, simply refined it. On 15 September, Ferenczi sends a curiously self-referential reply:

> I was and still am immersed in extremely difficult 'clarification work' – internal and external, as well as scientific – which has not yet produced anything definitive. . . The scientific aspect still centres around questions of technique, but its elaboration also reveals many points of theory in a somewhat different light. In my usual manner, I do not shy away from drawing out their conclusions to the furthest extent possible – often to the point where I lead myself 'ad absurdum'. But this does not discourage me. I seek advances by new routes, often radically opposed, and I still hope that one day I shall end up finding the true path. All this sounds very mystical: please don't be alarmed by this. As far as I can judge myself, I do not overstep (or only seldom) the limits of normality. It's true that I am often wrong, but I am not rigid in my prejudices.
>
> (Diary, pp. xiv–xv)

In October, the Ferenczis spend a vacation at the Hotel Quisisana on the island of Capri, off Naples. Ferenczi writes to Groddeck:

> I am honestly trying to put myself together again after that major intellectual and physical fatigue. For the first time for years, I am on holiday without my patients. As for science: I plague myself with the nature of trauma. The splits [Zersplitterungen] even atomization of the personality pose a stimulating but complex set of enigmas to resolve. This brings us dangerously close to the problem of death (the mentally sick are really half-dead people). (10 October)

The same day, Ferenczi also writes to Freud, asking him to clarify those points Freud feels 'do not appear capable of leading to any desirable goal'.

Freud and Ferenczi get a chance to discuss this on 27 October, when the Ferenczis stop in Vienna for a few days on their way home from Capri. They review their differences, and Ferenczi promises to rethink his position. On 5 December, he writes to Freud to report that he is unable to controvert any of his new findings and equally incapable of changing his present psychoanalytic technique. On 13 December, Freud replies in his sternest tones yet (though the letter begins '*Lieber Freund*' – 'Dear Friend'). He disputes the role of Ferenczi's purported 'kissing technique' (*Küsstechnik*) in Ferenczi's new 'mutual analysis'. The notion that Ferenczi indulges in kissing patients derives in fact from one of his 'mutual analysands', Clara Thompson, who tells numerous people including Freud that 'I am allowed to kiss Papa Ferenczi as often as I like' (Diary, pp. 2–3). Understandably, this gives Freud cause for concern. 'You are to hear from the brutal fatherly side an admonition. . .according to my recollection, a tendency to sexual play with patients was not completely alien to you in preanalytic times, so that the new technique could be linked to an old error. That is why I spoke in my last letter of a new puberty' (Freud to Ferenczi, 13 December). Not surprisingly, Ferenczi is wounded by this, particularly by the reference to Elma. On 27 December, he replies:

> Your fear that I might develop into a second Stekel is unfounded. [Stekel was commonly assumed to indulge frequently in sexual relations with his patients – ed.] 'Sins of youth', mistakes, once they have been overcome and analytically worked through, can even make one wiser and more prudent than people who have never experienced such storms. My highly ascetic 'active therapy' was surely a pre-emptive device against such tendencies, which is why it assumed, by its exagger-

ation, a compulsive character. As soon as I realized this, I relaxed the rigidity of the restrictions and frustrations to which I had condemned myself (and others). Now I believe that I am capable of creating a congenial atmosphere, free from passion, which is best suited to draw forth what has previously been concealed. . . After overcoming the pain caused by the tone of our correspondence, I cannot but express the hope that our personal understanding as friends and scientists has not been disrupted by these developments – or, rather, that it will soon be restored.

(p. 4)

1932

On 17 January, Ferenczi starts his 'clinical diary' in which he reports on his sessions, often with theoretical and technical questions in mind. The correspondence with Freud becomes infrequent and dispirited. On 12 May, Freud writes: 'In the past few years you have withdrawn into isolation. . .but you must leave that island of dreams which you inhabit with your fantasy-children, and once again join in mankind's struggles' (p. xvi). He suggests that becoming President of the IPA will force Ferenczi out of this 'isolation'. It is the term 'fantasy-children' that strikes Ferenczi as particularly harsh, because it conflates his present patients with the children he could not have with Gizella and once longed to have with Elma. On 19 May, Ferenczi focuses on choice of vocabulary: 'when I refer to my present activity in terms of "a life of dreams", "day-dreaming", and a "crisis of puberty", this does not mean that I admit I am ill. In actual fact, I have the feeling that out of the relative confusion many useful things will develop and have already developed' (ibid.). Things come to a head over the issue of the IPA Presidency. On 21 August, ten days before the Wiesbaden Congress, Ferenczi withdraws his offer to stand for the post. Efforts by Freud, Eitingon and Brill fail to change his mind. Jones agrees to stand for President instead.

Between 28 and 30 August, Ferenczi visits Freud to read him the final version of the 'Confusion of tongues' that he intends to present at the Wiesbaden Congress in September. Freud asks Ferenczi not to give the paper at the Congress, and under no circumstances to publish it within a year, so that he has time 'to recognize in further work the technical incorrectness of . . .[his]. . .results' (Freud to Ferenczi, 22 October, Masson, 1986, p. 172). Ferenczi accedes to neither request and is deeply shocked and dejected by the meeting (letter to Freud, 27 September). Brill, Eitingon, and van Ophuijsen want to ban Ferenczi's paper, but Jones claims to stop them with the argument that 'it would be so offensive to tell the most distinguished member of the Association, and its actual Founder, that what he had to say was not worth listening to, that he might well withdraw altogether in dudgeon' (Jones, 3, p. 185). Finally, the Ferenczi paper opens the Congress and is published in the *Zeitschrift* (1932, 18, pp. 239ff.), but not in the English *International Journal of Psycho-Analysis*.

After the Congress, the Ferenczis visit the Groddecks in Baden-Baden, then continue to Biarritz, France, for a holiday. Ferenczi is suffering from extreme fatigue and his health is deteriorating rapidly. It is discovered that he has pernicious anaemia and he is prescribed liver extract. His condition improves in December. The last entry in his 'clinical diary' is dated 2 October, but he continues analysis with patients until Christmas.

1933

His condition worsens in the New Year and he has difficulty walking and breathing. In February, he retires to bed and slowly loses the use of his limbs. At 2:30 p.m. on Monday, 22 May, he dies suddenly from a paralysis of the respiratory system caused by the anaemia. He is buried on 24 May at the Farkasret Jewish Cemetery in Budapest.

Afterwards

Ferenczi's pupils have a major impact on psychoanalytic work throughout the world: first of all, in Hungary, where Vilma Kovacs then Imre Hermann continue Ferenczi's work (cf. Hermann, 1946); in France, where Eugénie Sokolnicka helps found the Société Psychanalytique de Paris; in Great Britain, through the work of Michael Balint, Ernest Jones, Melanie Klein and John Rickman; in the United States, through Franz Alexander, who founds the Chicago School in 1932; Sándor Rado, who helps found the Columbia University Psychoanalytic Clinic in 1946; Geza Roheim, who directs research at the New York Institute (cf. Dadoun, 1972, pp. 57–9); Clara Thompson, who helps Karen Horney, Erich Fromm and Harry Stack Sullivan found the Association for the Advancement of Psychoanalysis in 1941 (cf. Thompson, 1943, 1950); and, finally, Margaret Mahler, Theresa Benedek, Sandor Lorand, Sandor Felman and Robert Bak.

Chapter 1

Premises

Ideas are always closely linked with the vicissitudes in the treatment of patients, and by these are either repudiated or confirmed.
—Sándor Ferenczi to Sigmund Freud, 10 December 1931

THIS IS UNASHAMEDLY an introduction to Ferenczi's work. It assumes, for good reason, that an English-speaking audience will know very little about this self-declared 'restless spirit. . .or *enfant terrible* of psychoanalysis' (3, p. 127). The last English 'edition' of his work was assembled in the 1950s from translations largely undertaken in the 1920s. Much of this now appears hopelessly dated and inaccurate. The edition is also incomplete, as many of the early Hungarian articles, some German lectures and most of his trenchant reviews remain untranslated. Finally, the work is not chronologically ordered, nor cross-referenced, nor edited sufficiently to explain the forgotten detail of faded debates.

This book, therefore, offers reparation. Most of Ferenczi's psychoanalytic work, including the *Clinical Diary* (1988) and much of his correspondence, was written originally in German, so I have referred all English translations to the original German, *Bausteine zur Psychoanalyse*, (4 vols, 1927–39). I have also consulted the French edition, which has been translated, extensively edited and chronologically ordered by associates of the *Coq Héron* group, Judith Dupont, Suzanne Hommel, Françoise Samson, Pierre Sabourin and Bernard

This (*Oeuvres complètes*, 4 vols, 1982). As my knowledge of Hungarian is limited, I have relied heavily on Claude Lorin's French summaries of the early Hungarian articles in *Le Jeune Ferenczi* (1983). I have included a glossary and commentary on those of Ferenczi's terms which are not readily comprehensible from general psychoanalytic debate and major source books (see pp. 193–201).

The main aim of this part of the exercise is to survey the range of Ferenczi's contribution to psychoanalysis and to provide basic information on those aspects of his work hitherto unavailable in English. Superficially this may appear a simple didactic exercise, designed to explain and secure Ferenczi's formative role in the development of psychoanalysis. In fact, such an exercise is rendered complex by the prominence of a traditional but empty rhetoric that surrounds him. It is still fashionable to pay homage to his 'greatness', while at the same time suggesting that this bears little or no relation to the contemporary state of psychoanalysis. This is particularly the case with his 'technical innovations'. Little has changed since Edward Glover proclaimed in 1940 that there was almost total unanimity against Ferenczi's 'devices', adding that they were 'fading out of technique in England' (Glover and Brierley, 1940, p. 92). Today, few psychoanalytic or psychotherapy training programmes list his publications or refer to his work. If, by chance, they do, it is usually in a historical context in which Ferenczi's 'insights' have been superseded by those of later generations, notably the Klein and Balint schools (cf. Haynal, 1988, p. 97; significant exceptions are provided by Chasseguet-Smirgel (1967), Cremerius (1983), Falzeder (1986), Gedo (1976) and Grunberger (1974)).

It will be argued here that such empty rhetorical 'praise' and bold claims about his 'influence' bear little relation to his actual work. The fact that some important texts have still to be edited and published, even in the original German and Hungarian, bears some responsibility for this. Crucial in this respect is the unpublished *Freud/Ferenczi Correspondence*, which casts invaluable light on both the development of Ferenczi's work and its relationship to the psychoanalytic movement as a whole. A more nebulous, but equally important, contribution to misreading has been the totally unsubstantiated assumption that Ferenczi 'influenced' the theories of his famous analysands and pupils. No one, as yet, has either provided a critical framework in which such 'influence' can be textually cross-referenced or examined the terms in which (counter)transferential dynamics may determine such a reading. This is particularly misleading in the case of comparisons between Ferenczi's and Abraham's supposed 'relative influence' on Melanie Klein, none of which seems to be the product of analytical enquiry (cf. Grosskurth, 1986, pp. 75–6).

So an added brief here will be to counter such rhetorical effects and cast light on the genealogy of Ferenczi's work, by providing an appropriate critical context in which to assess both developments in his work and their relation to (counter-) transferential dynamics. Obviously this requires a biographical approach that is sensitive to the kinds of narrative interpretation that occur in psychoanalysis. A major problem here is that there is neither a 'classic' Ferenczi biography from which to work nor the kind of critical glossary that complements Freud studies (Bourguignon *et al.*, 1989). To fill this gap, therefore, I included the foregoing curriculum vitae, which incorporates hitherto unpublished information from archive sources. Unfortunately, much of this can be referenced by date and source only, as there are no other forms of index. This is particularly difficult in the case of the massive *Freud/Ferenczi Correspondence* (1908–32), as sev-

eral copies of this exist and a comprehensive edition is un-
likely to appear within the next five years. The text referred
to here is the copy held at the Freud Museum in London,
which was edited by Michael Balint. I have detected some
inaccuracies in this, and indicate them here where necessary.
All the translations are my own. None the less, it should be
stressed that this curriculum vitae is intended only as one
possible, and limited, response to the main psychoanalytic
questions posed about biography in the text: where, for
example, to set limits to time, space and interaction in any
psychoanalytic exercise? How to define developmental
phases, and movements between them, notably regression?
How to delineate the operation and accuracy of memory?
How to account for and represent special temporal phenomena like repetition, déjà vu or premonition? To some extent,
these questions vitiate the obvious need to establish introductory guidelines, to summarize and present formulae. The
approach here will be to reflect on such questions in different
contexts, including the chronological and the formulaic
(glossary) ones. The epistemological shifts and contradictions that occur will then be used to cast light on the development and elaboration of variant psychoanalytic narratives.

One of the major paradigms I want to test is that of
Ferenczi as the 'left-wing' or 'political Freudian' analyst (Jacoby, 1983). Many assumptions rule here, but few genuine
insights. It is common, for example, to label him a 'bol-
shevik' and associate him with the later generation of Marx-
ist analysts, Reich, Fromm and Fenichel (Jones, 1956, 2,
p. 87). The major supporting evidence usually given for this
is the university chair of psychoanalysis he was given in 1919
purportedly by Bela Kun's Revolutionary Council. In fact,
the chair was previously established by the liberal republican
Count Károlyi, but came into effect only under the Kun

regime. Furthermore, Ferenczi's previous political commitment had been orientated around intellectual review-groups like *Huszadik Század* (Twentieth Century) and *Nyugat* (West), which had no specific political affiliation but proposed a general attack on the ruling right-wing, Hungarian cultural independence from Austria and Germany, and advocated sexual liberation. In short, Ferenczi's political commitment originated and developed on the left, but actually distanced itself from Marxism. Its main aim was to revolutionize psychoanalysis, so as to revolutionize society. As he put it to Freud: 'I don't wish to "reform" society, really, I am not paranoid. I only want to free *thought* [*Gedanken*] and *discourse* [*Rede*] from the constraint of useless inhibitions in the relationship between people who are psychoanalytically orientated' (letter to Freud, 3 October 1910, underlined in original).

His first political task within psychoanalysis, therefore, was to outline the 'inhibitions' within which it operated. This meant tracing for analysts and patients the outlines of the power structures to which they were bound by unconscious paranoia.

> In the end insight into the *paranoia* of authority (God is insane, the world is chaotic). Realization: my paranoia (as analyst) is only the imitation (representation) of his, that is, of the powerful adult's. From now on: I have to detach myself (from patients) calmly, then perhaps cure them (teach them insight). Special task: to free the patients whom psychoanalytic paranoia has reduced to the status of minors, made dependent and permanently attached, truly to liberate them, *from us as well.*
>
> (*Diary*, pp. 160–1, original italics)

He centered his political critique, therefore, on an analogy between the analyst and the 'powerful adult', that is, the father, mother, teacher or priest. If you occupied any of these positions, you automatically assumed their authority and their supposed special hold on 'knowledge'. Your patient, therefore, or your child or pupil expected you to know and to relieve them of their doubts or pain by putting them in the picture and administering the right treatment. For Ferenczi, this position was obviously open to abuse; in fact, most abuse was at least sanctioned if not structured by this authority structure. Doctors, parents, teachers and priests used their power and authority to seduce, and much of this passed unnoticed, because the recipients, the powerless, found it hard to question the power and authority structures in which they lived. If you were a child who was raped by a parent, it was hard to escape the force-field that legitimated everything parents do; it was much easier to take the fault upon yourself and assume guilt. It was the same with doctors, teachers, priests and analysts: anything lethal could take its course as long as the appropriate societal support was provided.

In this respect, I think Ferenczi's view of the political role of psychoanalysis is quite anarchic[1]. It advocates discrediting the support that certain forms of psychoanalytic 'knowledge' give to paranoid structures, and replacing it with 'mutualism', or 'liberation' from the dependencies that derive from the unconscious dynamics of transference and countertransference (including those operating through 'interpretation'). Furthermore, he proudly preaches the unmitigated iconoclasm of the 'enfant terrible': '"Enfants terribles" are in revolt (perhaps to an extreme) against hypocrites, and exaggerate simplicity and democracy. Really favourable development (optimum) would lead to the development of individuals (and a race) that would be neither mendacious (hypocritical), nor destructive' (*Diary*, pp. 149–50; Ferenczi, 3, p. 127). This, in turn, justifies a general attack on received 'wisdom' and grand liberal gestures in analysis. He argues that it is no good just glossing over issues by changing the names or prefacing everything said with an escape clause; substituting, for example, the term 'analysand' for 'patient', 'facilitator' for 'analyst' or 'teacher', without actually cognizing the underlying power situation (cf. *Diary*, pp. 1–3).

Ferenczi's alternative is to accept that psychoanalysis is bound to operate within numerous interlocking power structures which it can neither easily negotiate nor subvert. People come to you as patients looking for doctors who 'know' and expecting some 'active' response. They are going to regress to infantile dependence and need some support. To argue then for a strategy which will totally frustrate such expectations and demands could be taken as cruel rejection, no matter how 'enlightened' the intent. Similarly, to relax people in the analytical session to the point where they come to see the analyst as the good breast machine that pumps out a regular 'fix' deprives them of both independence and the chance to discover what really oppresses them. Ferenczi therefore argues for multiple and variant psychoanalytic techniques, which can be applied flexibly according to the context.

Clearly, this just negotiates the vicissitudes of power in analysis and does not fundamentally alter them. Ferenczi believes that general acceptance of 'lay', or non-medical, psychoanalysis can upset if not subvert the perceived *status* of the analyst, though he recognizes that gains here will be superficial. Deeper transformation relies on the creation of favourable conditions through analytical flexibility. He gives this transformation process several titles: 'active method', 'relaxation technique' and 'mutual analysis'. These all incorporate various degrees of self-conscious power manipulation into psychoanalytic technique. There are no fixed rules for this. It can include analysts seeking to exploit positive trans-

ference to gain agreement for the patient's self-imposed control of compulsive activity such as masturbation; offering
ad hoc autobiographical insights to the patient; even allowing the patient to assume the role of analyst when appropriate. In all of this, it is argued, the principal paradigm is an
anarchic 'mutual aid': it replaces the one-way process in
which the analyst *observes*, then offers a diagnosis of the
patient, with a two-way *co-operative dialogue*.

Without appreciating, or judging, either 'active' or
'mutual' analysis at this stage, it is important to see how they
shift the analytical balance from the transference to the countertransference. Ferenczi insists that the two cannot be separated. The analyst's interpretations cannot be immunized
from countertransferential elements, which in turn need to be
analysed at some point for patients, that is, in relation to
their transference. The 'supervision' of analytical sessions is
therefore essential, but does not remove the responsibility of
bringing the countertransference into the analytical process
itself.

It is not difficult to see, then, how in this way Ferenczi has
politicized psychoanalytic terminology, as well as any debate
surrounding it. It is also not difficult to appreciate how this
politicization has infiltrated discussion on technique: on the
play mode of child analysis, for example, which can be seen
to connote democratic dialogue, rather than the more au-
thoritarian 'educative' monologue approach. Similarly,
'focal' or brief methods of analysis connote awareness of
working-class and public service budgets, unlike the *laissez-
faire* approach of five times a week, for however long it takes,
which suits exclusively the independently wealthy.

The problem here is how to reflect adequately this politicization in the context of an introduction to Ferenczi's work.
Any straight line-up of his conceptual models would miss the

playful and extempore dynamic of his work: take, for example, Frank Sulloway's singular concern for accuracy, consistency and unilinear progression in 'psychoanalytic thought' (1979, pp. 379-81). This leads him to marvel at Ferenczi's 'highly fanciful' thesis that everyone mirrors the great global catastrophes in their development and progresses from the sea floor to the ice-age mountains. There is little point, he suggests, in considering such daft outmoded evolutionary theory unless, perchance, one is concerned with the gothic excesses of late-nineteenth-century scientific imagination.

In rebuttal, Ferenczi's defenders traditionally argue that it is inappropriate to judge these theories on the level of fact. Ferenczi simply used them metaphorically to evoke imaginitive features of the infant's inner world (cf. Sabourin, 1985, pp. 160-82). This view owes much to Michael Balint's celebrated apologia: 'His scientific language', Balint admitted, 'is indeed horrifying to any purist or would-be translator. For Ferenczi, words and technical terms were only – more or less – useful means of expressing mental experience' (1949, p. 216).

In fact, neither of these points of view is mutually exclusive. Ferenczi may well have intended such a journey from sea to mountain both to be taken literally and to prime an analogy for travel in the inner world. It is not crucial therefore to separate its registers of fact and fantasy. Unlike the imaginary big bad world of empirical science, psychoanalytic theories do not need to pass a verification test before they are admitted into a clinical session. Instead, they work or fail according to their evocation of unconscious processes. So the journey from ocean floor to ice-age mountains may simply serve as a 'useful fiction', a convenient narrative form to map out the patient's and analyst's shared hidden and hazardous routes through the psychoanalytic terrain.[2] In this context, therefore, it is of secondary importance whether contemporary biologists judge the journey's evolutionary connotations to be 'crazy'.

In contrast to both these views, therefore, this book aims rather to approximate the psychoanalytic process itself, and transform the narrative to accomodate the levels on which interpretation operates. To do this, I propose to follow Ferenczi's own method of 'utraquism'. He describes this as follows:

> To bring some light to bear critically on the manner in which our present-day science works, I was compelled to assume that, if science is really to remain objective, it must work alternately as pure psychology and pure natural science, and must verify both our inner and outer experience by analogies taken from both points of view; this implies an oscillation between projection and introjection. I called this the 'utraquism' of all true scientific work.

> (2, p. 373)

Ferenczi's main point about analogies is that they negotiate the inability of any philosophy to rid itself of the subjective and erect a purely objective view of the world. No matter how 'strict' the science, its analogies rely on the subjective dynamics of projection or introjection. No matter which language or medium we employ to relate to objects, it is impossible to isolate an outer from an inner world in which mutual products proliferate. A useful illustration of this is Ferenczi's analysis of the machine analogy. He argues here that machines should not be viewed exclusively as autonomous objects operating according to their own laws in the external world. This would ignore the psychic processes that are integral to their construction and operation. Instead, machines negotiate the difficult relationship between the psyche and the external world, hence develop different structures and functions to secure and foster psychic growth. 'There really are *primitive* machines', he explains,

> that do not yet signify projections of organs but *introjections* of a part of the external world by means of which the sphere of influence of the ego is enlarged – thus the stick or hammer. The self-acting machine, on the other hand, is already almost a pure *organ projection*; a part of the external world is 'given soul' [*begeistet*] by human will and works instead of our hands. The introjection and projection machines – as I should like to call them – do not therefore exclude one another; they only correspond to two developmental stages in the conquest of reality.
>
> (2, p. 390)

The machine analogy therefore mutually contains the metaphor-machine and object-machine in a two-way psychic movement, intro- and pro-jection; this movement, in turn, is also integrated into the machine analogy.

The challenging point in this formulation of analogy is the way in which the tension between introjection and projection is resolved by 'developmental stages in the conquest of reality'. Clearly, as just noted, this relies on a vitalist philosophy whose principal tenet has long since been disproved, namely that each individual recapitulates the development of the species. None the less, 'development' can still be considered as an analogy that displays all the metaphoric and metonymic tension contained in Ferenczi's representation of the psychoanalytic process. It can act as a container for the different narratives that Ferenczi believed formed psychoanalytic time and space.

It thus seems appropriate to structure this introduction to Ferenczi along the developmental lines of this analogy. This facilitates an examination both of the limitations of his 'scientific exposition' and of the associated metaphorical space generated within the psychoanalytic situation.

The next chapter therefore examines the whole 'project' of development: that is, how Ferenczi analyses time and relates it to spatial progression. Central here is the status of memory and the problem of narration of the past.

The third chapter looks at 'foreplay', or the processes which supposedly prime such development. Temporal and spatial metaphors figure prominently again here, notably in the representation of 'preparatory phases' (such as the latency period) and of appropriate body-sites (oral, anal, phallic and genital).

The fourth chapter moves on to the declared aim of development, namely 'coitus'. In Ferenczi's view, the major feature here is that the act may succeed on one level, the continuation of the species, but is doomed to fail on another level, that is, the negotiation of a return to primal unity. The coital metaphor therefore contains the diverse sexual drives that persist from previous phases, which none the less fail to transform themselves or to dissolve, so continuously fragment. Here again Ferenczi analyses this in the temporal and spatial terms of rhythm and the body-location of affect.

The fifth chapter examines 'love', or what Ferenczi considers psychoanalysis can achieve 'after the act'. Important here is the power and status of psychoanalytic 'knowledge'. He argues that this does not contain simply 'intellectual insight' (*Einsicht*), but also 'experience' (*Erlebnis*), which is mediated affectively through the physical sense of well-being and strength.

The final chapter considers what the development analogy fails to convey within its generation of metaphorical space. Ferenczi typically labels this 'teratoma', a term which dramatically stems both physical and fictional extremes: in medical languages, a 'teratoma' denotes a tumour, whereas, in literary parlance, it captures a monster of the Mr Hyde or Frankenstein kind. Ferenczi uses the term to intimate that all our attempts to regain primal unity generate a supplement of metaphoric space, which gradually accretes into a twin being. The temporal and spatial definition of such 'beings' can assume fulsome dimensions: psychosomatic prompting of cancerous growths, for example, or psychotic 'twin' personalities that commit violent crimes.

To conclude, we will weigh up the instruments and procedures that psychoanalysis offers to operate on such teratomae. In fact, it is quite a limited choice. One can agree to 'cut', which, in the Freudian model, metaphorically re-opens castration wounds. For this, sharp phallomorphic scalpels are prescribed. Alternatively, one follows the late Ferenczi and proposes a nourishing diet that regenerates and replaces deficiencies. Here the procedure is more protracted and 'tender', if not painless. For this, the analyst requires something softer and rounder, that sufficiently approximates the mother's breast.

Chapter 2

Project

In analysis it is not legitimate to suggest or hypnotize things into *the patient, but it is not only right but advisable to suggest them* out.

—Sándor Ferenczi, 1931, 3, p. 134

SINCE ITS INCEPTION, psychoanalysis has been beset with problems of forging adequate explanatory models for time. At first, it was often assumed that these problems were peculiar to Freud, who passed them on to analysis as a whole. Hitschmann, for example, in his proselytizing study, *Freud's Theories of the Neuroses* (1921) stressed Freud's innovation in focusing on the amnesias in full conscious life rather than the curative ideal of full memory recall under hypnosis. 'The psycho-analyst can only wonder', he remarked, 'how the smooth and exact clinical histories of hysterical cases are produced by other authors' (Hitschmann, 1921, p. 196). The last vestiges of this view were destroyed in the 1950s and 1960s, with Jacques Lacan's inspired work on the complexity of Freud's view of temporal structures (Lacan, 1977, p. 48), and Laplanche and Pontalis's revisions of this in the context of the historical development of psychoanalytic conceptions of time (Laplanche and Pontalis, 1980; Laplanche, 1970, 1989; Pontalis, 1968). It is now clear that Freud's views on time were not unique, nor unilinear, nor consistent. They were formulated in the context of debates on the aetiology of hysterical phenomena and borrowed generously from other specialists and other languages, particularly the French School who could claim eminence in this area (M. Stanton, 1991). Furthermore, Freud was neither the only psychoanalyst who was building time models nor the first one: Jung, for example, pioneered the 'word-association' model, which both won adherents independently of psychoanalysis and helped tranform Freud's own views of the subject.

This contextualization of psychoanalytic discussion of time also needs to be extended to Ferenczi, whose individual contribution is sometimes masked by the label of 'Freud's disciple'. Ferenczi's early work, particularly on reflexes, was not rendered redundant by this encounter with Freud in 1908; neither was his later work conducted exclusively under Freudian premises (Ferenczi, 1901; cf. Lorin, 1984, p. 119). Indeed, he opened up his own fresh and fertile research areas, notably in the sexualization of language, the study of regression and clairvoyance. He was also central in introducing outside specialist debates into the heart of psychoanalytic enquiry (cf. his critique of Ernst Mach, 1919, 2, pp. 383ff.). Freud went so far as to suggest in 1933 that these innovations had 'gradually distanced' Ferenczi from the psychoanalytic 'circle' (Freud, 13, pp. 367ff.).

In general terms, the psychoanalytic debate on the problem of time can usefully be divided into three main areas of enquiry. First, there are basic epistemological questions raised by the perceived challenge of the 'unconscious' to conceptions of a linear temporal flow. These focus on which psychic agency can be said to 'perceive' time and how any accuracy can be attributed to such perceptions. Crucial in this is discussion of memory and its possible distortion by unconscious repression.

Second comes a range of questions around the issue of 'normal' development: how to refine accounts of transition from infancy to adulthood to include the smallest detail. A central difficulty here is the correlation of the oedipal development model with one of supposed psychosomatic progression. At its most simple, this suggests a culturally prescribed route through the dangerous rapids of incest and patricide, accompanied by delights that are equally prescribed to appropriate body-sites, the oral, the anal and the genital. At its most complex, more routes are mapped following different initial sexual positions, whose logic renders the 'normality' of the Oedipus complex problematic. These routes too incorporate more body-sites, such as the urethral/phallic and inner vaginal (Kestenberg, 1975).

A third, related area of enquiry concerns the problem of defining direction in time. The central paradox here lies in integrating a model of 'unconscious' processes that continue automatically, such as sleeping/waking or ageing, with an object-related model which allows the subject some freedom of directional choice, notably in the course of psychoanalysis. Accounts of the two major time-shapes at play here, regression and repetition, tend to radical polarization: either supposed 'automatic' phenomena like sleep, ageing and even insanity are explained as regressions or freedom of choice is given major if not imperial power over the somatic realm. On the phylogenetic, or 'direction of the species' level, this polarization is even more dramatic: either, as Ferenczi argued, the direction of the whole human race was regressive or the choice of sublimation negotiated the triumph of culture over nature (Ferenczi, *Thalassa*, pp. 83–5).

THE UNCONSCIOUS AND
LINEAR TEMPORAL FLOW

In the first, epistemological, area of enquiry, Ferenczi, like all the early psychoanalysts, related primarily to the hypnotic model for the treatment of hysteria. There were two main variants to this model: the first was formulated by the Charcot School in Paris and the second by the Bernheim School in Nancy. The former argued that hysterical symptoms were caused by the persistence in the unconscious of unresolved, powerful reactions to past trauma. The aetiology of the symptoms varied according to the trauma, but their temporal articulation relied on the intrusion of unconscious obsessional structures, or *'idées fixes'*, into consciousness. The subject therefore suffered a diminution of consciousness (*abaissement du niveau mental*) when these obsessional structures followed their unconsciously prescribed circularity by endlessly repeating themselves (*automatisme de répétition*). The physician could only hope to influence this 'repetition compulsion' (*Wiederholungszwang* or *contrainte de répétition*) by gleaning information about the split-off traumatic material while the subject was in a trance state. Sometimes this could then be re-introduced to the subject when conscious, thus supposedly undermining the obsessional structure. In contrast, the Bernheim approach argued that the unconscious material could be accessed at psychic levels other than the unconscious by using a technique called 'suggestion'. This involved relaxing the subject to various levels, ranging from half-sleep and day-dream to deep hypnosis, then asking them direct questions or giving them direct orders to uncover and remove the obsessional structures.

In the 1890s, a fierce debate raged between the two schools following a spate of criminal cases of murder, rape and robbery in which subjects claimed they had acted under the influence of 'suggestion' administered in music-halls, fairgrounds and circuses (Miller, 1975). The Bernheim School argued that this was perfectly plausible, whereas the Charcot School dismissed the claims as fraudulent. They believed that such trance states demanded a pathological basis, and that, even then, subjects could not actively carry out crimes, because the necessary temporal direction existed only in consciousness. Instead, they would lapse and repeat the hysterical symptoms. Of course, governments and legal professions were disinclined to take chances, so followed Bernheim's thesis and restricted the use of suggestion to medical practitioners.

Medics themselves had more room to manoeuvre and were more concerned with the efficacy of the diagnosis and cure than with crime prevention. In their different ways, both Ferenczi and Freud proposed subtle negotiations of the differences between Charcot and Bernheim in their personal practices. Freud was both Charcot's and Bernheim's German translator and tried, as far as possible, to maintain an academic and distanced balance between the two. This distance was formalized in 1897, when he revised psychoanalytic technique around the role of fantasy in memory and established the new procedure of 'free association'. His 'certain insight that there are no indications of reality in the unconscious' (21 September 1897, Freud and Fliess, 1985, p. 264) undermined the Charcot view of the accuracy of evidence of traumatic material recounted in trance states. Likewise, free association, or the invitation to patients to recount whatever came into their heads, countered the directive thrust of Bernheimian 'suggestion'.

Ferenczi did not follow this approach. On the contrary, he was strongly committed to Bernheim's method, though appreciative of the usefulness of Janet and the Charcot School's sophisticated diagnostic terminology (Ferenczi, 'Charcot', 1925; 'A hipnózis gyógyito értekéröl', 1904). Prior to his discovery of Jung's 'word-association' test in 1907, he was an ardent hypnotist. His study of hysterical materialization, particularly psychosomatic anaesthesia, was heavily reliant on Janetian formulations (Ferenczi, 2, p. 110). Even after his meeting with Freud in 1908, these interests continued, though modified by the free associative method. For most of his psychoanalytic career, 'suggestion' remained the primary model against which he defined his principal technical innovations (Ferenczi, 1, p. 54, pp. 58ff., 81, 271; 'Psychoanalysis and suggestion', 1912, 2, pp. 55ff., 184, 200, 212; 3, pp. 111ff., 134, 254–5, 269–70). Central to this was his opposition to the principle of psychoanalytic 'inactivity' which justified itself by appeal to scientific objectivity and neutrality. In his view, severely regressed patients did not need guarantees of the scientific integrity of the analyst's interpretations, but genuine affective support and nourishment. In some cases, this meant active intervention, such as recommendations and prohibitions, in the manner of Bernheimian 'suggestion'; in others, it meant soothing, relaxing and even touching the patient, similar again to the hypnotic methods of massage.

Common to all diagnoses of hysteria was the problem of biological and cultural 'origins' (Laplanche, 1989, pp. 21ff.). Both Ferenczi and Freud initially adopted a thesis, fashionable at this time, that biological origins not only preceded cultural ones, but structured them. Consequently, 'protista', or living matter reduced to its basic structure, was reflected in the 'animalcule', the fundamental human structure, which in turn was reflected in the cultural 'ego'. This intimates both an ultimate hereditary growth structure and an explanation of all ego malfunctions as 'degenerations' within this. All forms of mental illness, for example, all criminal activity, suicides and supposed 'perversions' like homosexuality and transvestism, were diagnosed as degenerate. The neatness and convenience of this formulation was hard to abandon, even though the evidence that emerged in psychoanalysis suggested a much more important role for the 'endo-psychic' (or purely psychological). The tension here is particularly evident in the development of Ferenczi's studies of homosexuality in the early 1900s; in 1902, he situated the aetiology of 'psychic sexuality' in the context of hereditary determinants (Ferenczi, '*Homosexualitas feminina*', 1902), but, by 1911, he had removed all reference to biological determination, and established instead homoerotic object choices 'charged with unsublimated "sexual hunger"' so that he could stress the endo-psychic aetiology of what he still considered a 'paranoid perversion' (Ferenczi, 'On the part played by homosexuality in the pathogenesis of paranoia', 1, pp. 184ff.; cf. Karsch-Haack, 1911).

The problematic relationship between biological and psychological 'origins' has therefore generated a hybrid narrative space in psychoanalysis. Laplanche and Pontalis have drawn attention to the peculiar 'middle ground' occupied by scenes that are supposed to transcribe the biological development of the species in the cultural development of the individual: the primal scene, the seduction scene, the castration scene and the return to the mother's breast (Laplanche and Pontalis, 1968; Laplanche, 1989). Clearly, it is the status of fantasy in these that renders their 'reality' problematic, though, conversely, that 'reality' is recuperated by the supposed 'orientation' these scenes structure into sexual object choice that ensures the continuation of the species. Today, of course, both these genetic and sexual orientation models have become outmoded. This, however, does not obscure their references to fantasy; in fact, one consequence of this outmodishness is to tip the balance from the biological to the cultural, so it has now become fashionable to discuss the status of scientific fantasy or the fantasy of origins (Gould, 1984).

THE PROCESS OF 'RECKONING'

Ferenczi was more committed to integrated biological/cultural structures than most of the early psychoanalysts, perhaps even including Freud himself. 'Psychoanalysis', Ferenczi wrote in 1926, 'like every psychology, in its attempts to dig to the depths must strike somewhere on the rock of the organic' (Ferenczi, 2, p. 377). He even regarded the survey of these particular depths as one of his special tasks within the psychoanalytic movement. In this respect, *Thalassa: A Theory of Genitality* (1924) is surely the epigram of this particular narrative form. Of this text, Freud wrote, 'it is the most daring application of psychoanalytic intuitions. . .to the biology of sexual processes, and even organic life. . .ever attempted'. He added, by way of qualification, that 'it would be vain today to wish to separate what we can admit as confirmed knowledge, from that which we try to guess about future knowledge by means of scientific fantasy [*Träumerei*]' (Freud, 1933c, 22, p. 229). Today, the temptation to treat such a text as a 'poem' is very great. Sabourin (1985), This (1986), Lorin (1983) and Revardel (1986), for example, treat its schematization of the great 'catastrophes' of onto/phylogenetic progression as a playful juxtaposition of various scientific models to cast light on general unconscious structures, including Ferenczi's own personal ones; their set comparison here is Jacques Lacan's use of mathematics and geometry to illustrate different aspects of the Lacanian corpus.

This approach unhinges Ferenczi's psychoanalytic technique from its orientation towards the 'real' organic, that is, the physical symptoms of his patients. The inadequacy of his perception of the organic neither reduces it to playful fancy nor does it negate the interpretative technique through which he narrates the organic. Ferenczi's psychoanalytic technique relied on a multiple determination. 'Psychic space', he argued, 'like physical space, has several dimensions, so that the site of a point in it can only be determined exactly by means of several axes' (Ferenczi, 1, p. 197). To erase one of the axes does not necessarily discredit the point.

In fact, one of Ferenczi's central methodological concerns was to define the impact between interpretation and determined structures like the (unconscious) organic. In line with his 'suggestion' model, this definition was 'active', involving complex negotiation of the affective space lying between conscious objective and unconscious determinations. He defined this complex negotiation as 'reckoning' (*Rechnen*), which carries commercial connotations of calculating and issuing bills.

When the tendency to set aside the surrounding world by means of repression or denial is given up, we begin to *reckon* [*rechnen*] with it, i.e. to recognize it as a fact. A further advance in the art of reckoning is. . .the development of the power to choose between two objects that occasion either more or less unpleasantness, or to choose between two modes of action that can result in either more or less unpleasantness. The whole process of thinking would then be such a work of reckoning – to a large extent unconscious, and interposed between the sensory apparatus and motility. In this process, as in modern reckoning machines, it is practically the result alone that comes into conscious view, while the memory-traces with which the actual work has been performed remain concealed i.e. unconscious. We can dimly surmise that even the simplest act of thinking rests on an indefinite number of unconscious reckoning operations, in which presumably every kind of arithmetical simplification (algebra, differential calculus) is employed; and that thinking in speech symbols represents the ultimate integration of this complicated reckoning faculty.

(Ferenczi, 2, p. 378)

Ferenczi's notion of 'reckoning', then, combines the discard through psychoanalysis of repression and denial of the external world, with a Charcotian innate and automatic self-regulatory mechanism of thought. This facilitates a mutually supportive, or co-operative, view of the development of the instruments of consciousness, such as language, and of the affective relationship of the individual to the outside world. This co-operation is fostered by 'autosymbolic' or 'functional' phenomena (a term Ferenczi borrows from Herbert Silberer).[3] These are defined as 'self perceptions that are symbolically represented', or 'those pictures occurring in dreams, fantasies, myths, etc. in which not the content of the thought and imagination, but the way of functioning of the mind (e.g. its ease, difficulty, inhibition etc.) is indirectly represented' (Ferenczi, 1, p. 261; Silberer, 1970).

These phenomena not only help represent the inner (unconscious) world, but are instrumental in 'reckoning' with the exterior world. Ferenczi consistently refers to three autosymbolic prototypes: the machine, the mirror and the bridge.

The machine negotiates the instrumental relationship between the body and the exterior world. 'The self-acting machine', he explains, '. . .is already almost a pure organ projection; a part of the external world is "given a soul" by the human will and works instead of our hands' (Ferenczi, 2, p. 390).

Similarly, the mirror negotiates our view of the external world's view of us. Diagnostically, then, the hysterical phobia of mirrors should be interpreted as the dread of self-knowledge, including its affective correlate of flight from the pleasures of looking and exhibitionism[4] (Ferenczi, 2, p. 365).

Finally, the bridge negotiates our psychic presence in the external world. It links our thoughts together, then links them to the external world. Word-bridges are the prototype of this autosymbolic phenomenon. Through connotation and denotation, words trace complex spatial and temporal patterns. Their position in sentences orientates temporal sequence and direction. Finishing sentences, for example, is an important analytic indication of the patient's sense of control and direction in the world. Similarly, the expression 'for example' often serves to bridge the gap between the general or remote and specific experience in which there is a clear direction (Ferenczi, 2, p. 185). Word-bridges even foster the useful conflation of words with the 'real thing', rendering it difficult to abandon the comforting belief that naming the world accurately mirrors and even controls it[5] (Ferenczi, 2, p. 355).

DEVELOPMENTAL REGISTERS AND BODY-SITES

The method of 'reckoning', regulated by 'autosymbolic phenomena', informs Ferenczi's views of the second area of enquiry into the nature of time: the problem of developmental models. He argues that the 'origin' of 'reckoning' engenders and structures the progression of subsequent development phases. The agency that is structured and fostered by 'reckoning' is the ego, whose parts and growth are autosymbolically 'linked' together by the language, mirror and bridge machines. This autosymbolic linkage, though, carries with it an exogenous dimension; the ego receives input and itself outputs into the external world. It follows, then, that the 'origin' of the ego structures an instrumental relationship with the outside that both predetermines its cultural shape (notably through language) and allows it sufficient time and space to develop its own trajectory, or manner of 'reckoning' (style).

The problem, then, is the relation with the biological origin which precedes this cultural one. Ferenczi's basic position is that pre-ego experience consists of un-mediated bodily sensations. These are lodged in the fragmented and 'inarticulate' sections of the nervous system which function 'allo- or auto-plastically' (see Glossary, p. 194; *Thalassa*, p. 72). This agency is called the 'Id' or 'It' (*Das Es*). 'Children in the first years of life. . .', he explains, 'have not many conscious memories of events, but only of sensations (pleasurable and un-pleasurable tones) and consequent bodily reactions. The "memory" remains fixed in the body and only there can it be awakened' (Ferenczi, 3, p. 269).

The difficulty here is, how do conscious, that is, ego-related memories differ from unconscious, that is, id-related 'memories'? For a time, Ferenczi played with Otto Rank's answer to this question, namely the notion that a primal birth trauma structured all future relations between the id and the ego. 'The essential part of the work of the analysis. . .', wrote Rank,

> is really neither more nor less than allowing the patient to repeat with better success in the analysis the separation from the mother. But this is by no means to be taken metaphorically in any way – not even in the psychological sense. For in the analytic situation the patient repeats, biologically, as it were, the period of pregnancy, and at the conclusion of the analysis – i.e., the re-separation from the substitute object – he repeats his own

birth for the most part quite faithfully in all its details. *The analysis finally turns out to be a belated accomplishment of the incompleted mastery of the birth trauma.*

(Rank, 1929, pp. 4–5, original italics)

Ferenczi was very attracted to this thesis for two reasons. First, it corresponded with some of his speculations on the ontogenetic recapitulation of phylogenetic development, namely that the intra-uterine state paralleled our original location in the sea (Ferenczi, *Thalassa*, pp. 44–45). Second, if it were true, it would justify the 'active' technique of directing interpretation towards uncovering this primal 'birth trauma' structure, thus considerably shortening the length of psycho-analysis. These reasons formed the bridge between Ferenczi and Rank in *The Development of Psychoanalysis* ([1922] 1986).

None the less, Ferenczi's attraction was weakened by two basic flaws in the formulation. The first was its reduction of temporal sequence to the repetition of a single set of birth events. The only justification for this was 'mastery' of the supposed primal and unique trauma. 'This cuts. . .[Rank] off. . .', Ferenczi argued, 'from the possibility of ever finding anything new: what he seeks and, of course, what he finds is only the confirmation of what he already knows. And further, it strikes me as inconsistent to deny the value of the historical standpoint in general, while at the same time laying such disproportionate weight upon the one particular histori-cal factor of birth' (Ferenczi, Review of Rank, 1927, p. 94).

Second, Rank's thesis focused exclusively on the mother, and inscribed all cultural as well as biological 'memories' within repetition of the expulsion from the womb. Ferenczi contended that this ignored the authority of the father in the oedipal dynamic and thus censored the identification of power and desire in the 'original' cultural scenarios of the primal scene, the castration scene and the seduction scene (Ferenczi, 1927, p. 97). Ferenczi could accept that *one* of the symbolic roles culturally prescribed for the phallus by the birth trauma was return to the womb (cf. Rank, 1929, pp. 38–9; Ferenczi, *Thalassa*, p. 50). However, there were other destructive roles, notably associated with the death-drive and castration, which Rank totally overlooked (Ferenczi, 2, p. 377).

Finally, Ferenczi came to the view that memory operates through both the ego and the id; the only difference between ego and id memories is their object-relatedness. Id memories are 'bodily sensations' which are located by primal life and death trends (*zugen*). When they are re-elaborated retrospectively (*nachträglich*) by the ego, they are experienced subjectively as emotions. Ego memories, by contrast, are 'projected sensations', that is 'sensations referred to the environment or "external events". As these are regulated autosymbolically, they appear as "objective", or verifiable by the instruments of consciousness' (Note of 26 October 1932, 3, pp. 260ff.). Their relationship to life and death trends is therefore more purposeful, and orientated through primal scenes. This sense of purpose is reflected in the term Ferenczi chooses to describe their object-relatedness; 'drives' (*Trieben*)[6] (*Thalassa*, p. 52). The crucial point here is that these different registers of memory interact. They assume different 'voices' in those registers that sometimes strike harmony and sometimes dissonance. They shift between emotion and objectivity, mix pleasure and pain or 'influence' the narration of the past through autosymbolic machines.

Ferenczi therefore regards discussion of the 'accuracy' of memory as an extremely limited topic. It concerns only the self-regulatory functions of the ego, as opposed to the wider issue of the ego–id relationship and its effect on time (or affect in time). At the end of his life, he gave great importance to the censorship that such an emphasis on 'accuracy' imposed on the wider functioning of memory. Rather romantically, he chose to do this by focusing on those memories whose balance lay to the id side of the ego–id mix. These memories he grouped together into 'the language of tenderness' (*die Sprache der Zärtlichkeit*), which he contrasted with the other, ego-dominated mix, which he called 'the language of passion' (*die Sprache der Leidenschaft*) (Ferenczi, 3, pp. 156ff.). The 'language of tenderness' conveyed 'the clear-sightedness of the uncorrupted child' (*Diary*, p. 81). By this, he did not mean that the child was incapable of 'perversions' following sado-masochistic trends (*Zugen*), simply that these were untrammelled by exogenous stimulation, therefore not passionate and guilt-laden like 'drives' (*Trieben*) (Ferenczi, 3, p. 166).

TEMPORAL DIRECTION

Ferenczi's approach to the third main area of enquiry into time, the problem of temporal direction, was based primarily on his view of the two registers of memory. In the interaction between ego and id memories, the ego develops an extra regulatory mechanism, the super-ego, to orientate itself effectively in the environment (Ferenczi, 'The adaptation of the family to the child', 1927, 3, p. 73). The super-ego navigates the ego through the oedipal rapids, past 'perverse' gratification to 'normal' sexual objects that do not disturb the continuation of families. Its main compass-point in this is incest, and its main forms of emotional articulation through the 'language of passion' are anxiety and guilt. Despite the power

of this agency, it is continuously subverted by the id memories, which deflect the compass-needle and insert the language of tenderness into the narrative of passion. As we have
seen, the language of tenderness has a different temporality
which is articulated by the body, so that breaks in the super-
ego's directional sense are manifested physically. These
breaks can be restorative, in so far as they restore the 'clear-
sightedness of an uncorrupted child': in this, Ferenczi views
sleep and coitus as 'positive' regressions, that both exclude
external stimulation and approximate to the foetus position[7]
(*Thalassa*, p. 72). Or they can be negative, in which case
'hysterical materialization' takes place: in this, the body articulates the conflict between the super-ego direction (*Trieben*)
and the id-based desire (*Zugen*).

The psychoanalyst, of course, is more likely to come into
contact with the negative rather than the positive breaks. It is
essential, then, to pick up the non-verbal cues, and appreciate the particular symbolic constellation in which they
operate[8] (K. Stanton, 1988). The main problem here is that
pure id memories cannot be accessed verbally, though later
ego-mediated ones may. The body pains of autistic patients,
for example, or chronic cases of hysterical anaesthesia may
be conceptualized but not treated psychoanalytically (Ferenczi, 2, p. 110). Once the ego incorporates an external
referent, however, the symbolic elaboration of the symptoms
through the body becomes potentially limitless and acces-
sible through psychoanalysis.

The symbolic elaboration of symptoms through the body
is articulated through the temporal forms negotiated between
the id and ego memories. As such, various body-sites relating
to different 'events' produced by different narratives can
combine in a single physical symptom. To illustrate this,
Ferenczi cites the example of a patient who came for treat-

ment for impotence. In fact, the man, displayed another, more troubling symptom, a peculiar form of constipation. This was frequent but irregular and involved acute pain in which he claimed to feel the stool form inside him. Even if he defecated, the pain would not disappear. Ferenczi uncovered a number of events that influenced this symptom. First, the man had been forced to marry by his father. Then it emerged that the constipation appeared whenever he came into conflict with a 'masculine personality who in any way impressed him'. Finally, homosexual drives and id-based memories imposed themselves:

> Just on the occasions when he wanted to make a determined stand against someone, he was prevented by an unconscious homosexual fantasy and with the help of the contractile rectal walls was compelled to mould for himself a male organ – the member of the consciously hated opponent – from the plastic material of the ever-present rectal contents that would not remove itself from the rectum till the conflict was solved in some fashion or other.
> ('The phenomena of hysterical materialization', 1919, 2, p. 95)

Ferenczi draws attention here to the impossibility of restricting this to one development 'phase', say the anal or genital one, since the drives associated with these phases influence each other and impinge on both the body rhythm (constipation) and the narrative of events (impotence). Likewise, the development of narcissistic ego formation around identification with the penis is displaced to anal functions and rhythm (stool formation). Ferenczi regards this displacement as a common feature surrounding the 'deferred action' (*Nachträglichkeit*) of narcissistic wounds. The 'lump in the throat' phenomenon (*globus hystericus*) or the imaginary pregnancy parallel the constipation case in other body-sites (2, pp. 95,

104–5). In many of these displacements, masturbation rituals are woven into the fantasy structure to defend the threatened ego. But even here, the super-ego imposes guilt and anxiety that further displaces the body location: nervous tics are a classic example of such displaced masturbation rituals ('Psychoanalytical observations on the tic', 1921, 2, pp. 142ff.).

CLAIRVOYANCE

A distinctive feature of Ferenczi's conception of time is the notion that ego development can actually distort and reduce the scope of existence. The ego's excursions into the exopathic generate set forms of symbolic distance from the spontaneous run of direct experiences. Similarly, its reliance on the illusions of control fostered by language and machines actually often blocks the natural life trends (*Zugen*) to such a degree that hysterical materialization sets in. In this respect, Ferenczi contrasts the problems of an over-intellectual ego with the 'clear-sightedness of the uncorrupted child'. The over-intellectual ego is dominated by 'the impulse to explain rationally by the external order of their world their own irrational inner strivings', hence delusionally attempts to close itself off to the language of tenderness (1, pp. 292–3). In contrast, infantile sexuality before the language of passion contains an unequalled directness and spontaneity. This is illustrated by the frequent adult dream scenario in which a baby suddenly bursts forth eloquently with great insight and wisdom ('The dream of the "clever baby"', 1923, 2, pp. 349ff.; 3, p. 136).

Ferenczi even goes so far as to claim that the power of clairvoyance can be explained in terms of regression to this infantile realm (*Diary*, p. 81; 2, pp. 249–50; 3, pp. 135–6, 165,

271–4). Curiously, Freud initially expresses extreme scepticism at this explanation, but, after a visit to the famous clairvoyant Frau Siedler in Berlin, has to retract his objections on the grounds that she was too 'exceptionally stupid and inactive a person' ever to be able to fake the evidence (unpublished letter from Freud to Ferenczi, 11 October 1909). Ferenczi subsequently advocates that psychoanalysis should fully explore this realm: 'Just think of this interesting discovery in the history of transference. . .', he writes to Freud, 'I am a wonderful clairvoyant [*Wahrsager*], that is a thought-reader! I read (in my free associations) the thoughts of my patients. The future method of psychoanalysis must draw from this' (letter from Ferenczi to Freud, 22 November 1910).

Ferenczi develops this insight into an 'orientation' for the progression of psychoanalysis. If ego intervention is restricted, then the transference will not be mediated autosymbolically, that is, distorted by repressed material, but actually convey the thoughts and emotions of the other. In this sense, he talks of thought transference (*Gedankenübertragung*) which can work somatically – pains, for example, can be transferred – as well as verbally, pictorially and even musically (letter from Ferenczi to Freud, 14 October 1909). Furthermore, this transference can inform analysts as to the direction they must take to remove the blockages imposed by the language of passion, and free the language of tenderness. 'A large part of children's sexuality is not spontaneous', he explains, 'but it is artificially grafted on by adults, through over-passionate tenderness and seduction. It is only when this grafted-on element is re-experienced in analysis, and is thereby emotionally split up, that there develops *in the analysis*, initially in the transference relationship, that untroubled infantile sexuality from which, in the final phase of the analysis, the longed-for normality will grow' (*Diary*, p. 75).

Obviously, such a concept of thought transference delves into the hotly disputed depths of debate on extra-sensory perception. It is not essential to enter into this here, simply to note how Ferenczi used it to support his case for the creation of a nurturing, trusting and co-operative environment in which such regression to the language of tenderness could occur. It is crucial to appreciate, however, that it led Ferenczi to believe not only that the analyst's regression was essential in order to foster this language, but also that he or she was bound in this process to confront their own language of tenderness. This tempered the 'unalleviated suffering' (*lenteszierendes Leiden*) imposed by contemptuous analysts with 'a salutary loss of illusions about oneself and thus to the awakening of a real interest in others' (*Diary*, p. 194). This 'real interest' therefore denied any end or closure to the process of analysis. 'I do not know of any analyst', he wrote, 'whose analysis I could declare, theoretically, as concluded (least of all my own). Thus we have in every single analysis, quite enough to learn about ourselves' (ibid.).

Chapter 3

Foreplay

Analytical experience makes it highly probable that many intelligent children at the stage of repression marked by the latency period, before they have gone through the 'great intimidation', regard adults as dangerous fools, to whom one cannot tell the truth without running the risk of being punished for it, and whose inconsistencies and follies therefore have to be taken into consideration. In this children are not so very wrong.

—Sándor Ferenczi, 1912, 1, pp. 203–4

'TRANSFERENCE' IS CLEARLY not only the most important but also the most hotly disputed psychoanalytic concept. On the one hand, it is claimed that '[the] use of the term. . .has on the whole been confined to psychoanalysis, and. . .should not be confused with the various psychological uses of "transfer"' (Laplanche and Pontalis, 1980, p. 455; cf. H. B. and A. C. English, 1958). In this sense, the function of 'transference' in the psychoanalytic treatment should be regarded as a *special* case, tailored to the desires and needs contained within the relationship between the patient and the analyst. On the other hand, it is often claimed that 'transference' is neither the exclusive property of analysis nor indeed is its projection of unconscious prototypes or 'imagos' on to others *primarily* found in analysis; romantic 'love', for example, is clearly a more popular model (cf. LaCapra, 1988). 'Love', in fact, in its mercurial production of new variants of the old story, continuously subverts the *special* quality that analysts would like to claim for transference phenomena in analysis.

It is curious that Freud is often cited to support both views. First, there is Freud's view that the analyst literally replaces the early figure who initially inspired the thoughts, sensations and emotions conveyed in the transference.

> [Transferences] are new editions or facsimiles of the impulses and fantasies which are aroused and made conscious during the progress of the analysis; but they have this peculiarity, which is characteristic for their species, that they replace some earlier person by the person of the physician. To put it another way; a whole series of psychological experiences are revived, not as belonging to the past, but as applying to the person of the physician at the present moment.
>
> —Freud, 1905, 7, pp. 157–8

Alternatively, there is the view, contained within *An Autobiographical Study*, that 'It must not be supposed. . .that transference is created by analysis and does not occur apart from it. Transference is merely uncovered and isolated by analysis. It is a universal phenomenon of the human mind, it decides the success of all medical influence, and in fact dominates the whole of each person's relations to his human environment' (Freud, 1925, 20, pp. 79–80).

What is missing in both views, and both supporting quotes, is any sense of the historical context in which the notion of transference developed. It is overlooked, for example, that the first quote comes from the 'Dora case', in which transference features as a 'postscript', precisely because Freud has missed its importance in structuring the course of the analysis. His observations are therefore inferred retrospectively, rather than developed within the procedure of the analysis itself. In the second quote, too, there is no sense of the rhetoric of this piece, which is designed to *situate* recent conflicts in the psychoanalytic movement within the terms of the transference dynamic. This is particularly the case in Freud's break with Jung, because Jung had previously played such a formative role in locating transference in a psychiatric context, notably by associating it with neurosis, as opposed to psychosis, in which introversion destroyed transferential relations with the external world (cf. Jung, 1972, 3, p. 190). Later, much to Freud's dismay, Jung shifted focus to portray 'real' transference as a spiritual bond that linked people to each other and to Christ in 'the miracle of redemption' (Jung, 1919, pp. 41ff.). Of course, this did not exclude supposed neurotic disturbance associated with such 'miracles', but it did impose on the general debate the question of the status of non-clinical parallels like 'love' and 'religious experience'.

Ferenczi's work on transference attempts to mediate between purely clinical and cultural definitions. This is not to say that he argues from the clinical to the cultural, or generally supports Freud's views. On the contrary, his early seminal article, 'Introjection and transference' (1909, 1, pp. 35ff.), intimates many future differences from Freud's 'Dora case' definition. First of all, Ferenczi insists that transference has to be understood in terms of object relations, and thus effectively can operate across a wide range of objects in a wide range of activities: choice of food, for example, or manner of cooking or particular political or religious preferences can indicate transference of 'repressed erotic (genital or coprophilic) inclinations' (ibid., p. 38). Second, these specific forms of object relation all operate through displacement: the colour of a person's hair, for example, the way they hold a cigarette or pen, their name, the tenor of their voice can articulate transference[9] (ibid., p. 42). Third, transference is structured around the fantasy 'scenes' which unconsciously prescribe perception: 'The first loving and hating', he contends, 'is a transference of auto-erotic pleasant and unpleasant feelings on to the objects that evoke those feelings. The first "object-love" and the first "object-hate" are, so to speak, the primordial transferences, the roots of every future introjection' (ibid., p. 49). In short, there are positive and negative forms of transference, which respectively nourish and attack the chosen object. Finally, these 'primordial transferences' can often later form a fixed focus, through oedipal dynamics, on the mother and father as objects of desire and hatred.

It is significant that Ferenczi attempts to prove this account of transference dynamics by reference to the hypnotism model. Hypnotism simply exploits the primordial transference structures which attach affect to objects. So there are two basic affective positions the hypnotist can exploit in order to gain access to the unconscious associations attached to the object: the first postion is modelled on the primordial father, so is stern and uses command to penetrate through the patient's consciousness; the second is modelled on the primordial mother, so is unconditionally nurturing and relaxes patients to the point where they willingly cede whatever gives rise to pain or unease (1, p. 54). Ferenczi's concern here is to indicate how both hypnotism and psychoanalysis tend to privilege the first position at the expense of the second. They identify with the authority of the father and forget about the love of the mother. Hence the affections generated within the transference are often negative and based on dread of the father, who projects his 'knowledge' into their vulnerable body of associations (*Thalassa*, p. 32). Analysts' 'insensitivity' (*Fühllosigkeit*) to this bias actually further complicates the patient's condition (cf. *Diary*, 7 January 1932, pp. 1ff). Another level of displacement is added to the original transferential one, and usually articulates itself through the patient's body. Ferenczi calls this 'ventriloquism' (*Bauch-reden*). Key illustrations of this are compulsive yawning, sighing and coughing in the analytical session, which 'ventril-oquize', or give 'separate voice', as it were, to the patient's anxieties (1, p. 209).

The suppression of the primordial mother's position in transference preoccupies Ferenczi's later meditations on psy-choanalytic technique (beginning, notably, with the famous paper on psychoanalytic 'abuses', 'On the technique of psy-choanalysis', 1919, 2, pp. 177–89). This focuses first of all on how such suppression can take place; second, on why ana-lysts are aften unable to occupy the nurturing, 'introjecting' mother's position. One reason for both is the 'icy reserve' that some feel guarantees the clinical respectability and academic impartiality of the analytic exchange. Of course, on the one hand, it is not difficult to define how the glacial approach misses something in the transference heat. To warm analysts up to the right temperature, Ferenczi proposes to unite the terms 'love' and 'hate' to 'transference': transference-love and transference-hate (*Übertragungsliebe/Übertragungshass*) (2, p. 290). On the other hand, it is harder to define how repres-sions operate within the analyst's input into sessions. This raises the complex issue of the 'countertransference', or the analyst's own transferential distortion of the analytical situa-tion; the complexity derives mainly from defining the inter-transferential dynamic, especially given Ferenczi's analogy here with clairvoyance (see p. 88).

Controversially, Ferenczi argues that psychoanalysis will not essentially differ from hypnotic suggestion if the counter-transference does not incorporate the primordial mother's position (2, p. 187). This does not mean foreclosing the pri-mordial father's position, simply refusing to let it foreclose the primordial mother's position in the inter-transferential dynamic. Effectively, this implies maintaining access through the dual primordial transference-track to the whole range of object relations. In short, the 'love' and 'hate' evoked can explore the range of channels between homo- and hetero-sexuality, and the corresponding emotional tension and release can heighten through 'active avoidance of somatic ventriloquism'. Analysis of the countertransference, therefore, provokes a psychosomatic 'greenhouse effect', that eventually dissolves into the integrity, trust and cure proposed by psychoanalysis. The only way of protecting and nurturing this kind of countertransferential input is to institute obligatory psychoanalysis of all psychoanalysts and to recommend constant supervision ('The elasticity of psychoanalytic technique', 1928, 3, pp. 88–9).

* * *

Transference originates and progresses through play (*Spiel*). This is now a familar, if controversial thesis, though in 1913, when Ferenczi first elaborated it systematically, it appeared to be dangerous pioneer work in an unknown territory ('Stages in the development of the sense of reality', 1913, 1, pp. 213ff.; 'A little chanticleer', 1913, 1, pp. 240ff.; 'Infantile ideas about the female genital organs', 1913, 2, pp. 314ff.; 'Childish ideas of digestion', 1913, 2, pp. 325ff.; 'The cause of reserve in a child', 1913, 2, pp. 327ff.; 'On the ontogenesis of symbols', 1913, 2, 1, pp. 276ff.). Of course, this work proved to inspire the future direction of child analysis, not least through Melanie Klein and Margaret Mahler, both of whom began their careers in Ferenczi's Budapest circle[10] (cf. Klein, 'Early stages of the Oedipus conflict and of super-ego formation', 1975, pp. 123ff.; Mahler, 1988, pp. 16–18). Furthermore, Ferenczi's extension of the notion of play to include language prefigured both Freud's 'fort-da' model in *Beyond the Pleasure Principle* (1920) and Lacan's subsequent 'mirror phase' (1966).

The main initial insight into play is that it operates the displacement demanded by the primordial objects in the first object relations. Play's *primum mobile*, or kick-start, occurs when the first 'malicious thing' obtrudes to forestall gratification, or even inflict pain (1, pp. 48–9). At this point, the 'interest' (*Vorteil*) is shifted from the denied gratification to the object. The 'feeling-drive' (*Gefühlstrieb*) is projected into the object, thus investing it with gratification affects. If the object continues to deny gratification or, in fact, inflicts pain, then it is invested with negative affects. In any case, there is a displacement (*Verschiebung*) which contains the particular mix of pleasure and pain; the displacement also incorporates affective fluctuation associated with the object (*Verschiebung* is consistently rendered as 'displacement' by Strachey, but can also connote 'fluctuation', 'dislocation' and 'transference'). 'Play' (*Spiel*) then negotiates the range and flexibility of displacement necessary to contain and eventually control affective fluctuation (*Spiel*, incidentally, does not necessarily need an ego to do this – the word also connotes the motion of a machine).

Ferenczi argues that transference play continuously displaces the site of gratification and denial. This play occurs in oral, anal and phallic/genital phases. In the oral, it is play with the nipple or sucking (*Lutschen*). Then, in the anal phase, the faeces become the infant's first 'toys' (1, p. 326). They serve as the first paint, and daub love and hate feelings on primal objects. Then play operates displacement through numerous symbolic registers: first, the introjected sense of smell (1, pp. 134, 143; 'Flatus as an adult prerogative', 1913, 2, p. 325; second, through obscene language and its coprophilic invocations ('On obscene words', 1911, 1, pp. 132ff.); finally, through the cultural coprosymbol of money ('The ontogenesis of the interest in money', 1914, 1, pp. 319ff.; 'Two typical faecal and anal symbols', 1915, 2, pp. 327ff.).

The first transference play within the oedipal dynamic is masturbation. Here incestuous desire for the parental objects is displaced through the primal and castration scenarios into masturbatory ritual. Ferenczi suggests here that such rituals symbolically re-incorporate the incest motif. In male masturbation, the hollow of the hand substitutes for the mother's vagina; in female masturbation, the finger substitutes for the father's penis (*Thalassa*, p. 23). Furthermore, homosexual drives frequently and fluctuatingly displace such identifications, usually through introjecting part or whole genital objects of the same sex or further displacing the ritual through anal eroticism (ibid., p. 24). There is also a biological structure that supports this bisexual 'play'; in women, the clitoris replicates the penis, and in men, the glans penis is invaginated and is contained within the foreskin which duplicates the enclosing function of the maternal womb (ibid., p. 28).

Of course, today, this biological thesis appears somewhat fanciful, though we can all accept that we contain various male and female physical components (chromosomes, hormones, etc.) and that sexual difference is not as distinct as once assumed. Anyway, Ferenczi's use of this thesis is *utraquistic*; it suggests only that it may provide productive analogies (see above, p. 64). Today, he would surely shift the analogies, though the bisexual function of transference play would remain the main reference. The most important feature of all this is the fusion of different eroticisms, containing different pleasurable and painful experiences, with different object relations and forms of displacement. Ferenczi labels this fusion '*amphimixis*', a medical term denoting the mingling of two different substances ('*amphi*', a Greek prefix, means 'on two sides'), whose main example is the fusion of sperm and ovum to create the foetus. He extends this meaning analogically to characterize the masturbatory play of children, which fuses different kinds of pleasurable activity in its rituals. Children, for example, combine thumb-sucking, nose-rubbing and ear-pulling in various ways; or they variously combine defecating and eating or genital stimulation and anal finger-play (*Thalassa*, p. 13). These are not always but often fusions from a dual source. Here is the prototype (elaborated some six years before Freud's fort/da version):

> The most characteristic example of an amphimictically urethro-anal performance I owe. . .to a two-year-old boy who would sit on a chamber and alternately pass a few drops of urine and a little faeces or flatus to the accompaniment of a continuous cry of '*egy csurr, egy pú–egy csurr, egy pú*, which may be translated into English, in the vernacular of childhood, as 'now a pee, now a poop'.
>
> (*Thalassa*, p. 14)

Ferenczi stresses that 'amphimixis' does not 'guide' sexual development by progressively displacing the site of gratification from the mouth to the anus to the genitals. On the contrary, it diversifies the sites and their symbolic combination through which erotic drives are expressed. One does not abandon early amphimictic structures, but elaborates further on them, especially utilizing new mastery gained through language. Furthermore, the transference play of amphimixis aims to defend against the primal 'malicious thing' and the anxiety associated with the primordial fantasy scenarios. As such, it constitutes a *foreplay*, which ritually precedes most sex acts to defend against the primordial negative transferences:

Psychoanalytic experience has established that the acts preparatory to coitus. . .have as their function the bringing about of an
identification with the sexual partner through intimate contact
and embraces. Kissing, stroking, biting, embracing serve to
efface the boundaries between the egos of the sexual partners, so
that during the sex act the man, for example, since he has as it
were introjected the organ of the woman, need no longer have
the feeling of having entrusted to a strange and therefore hazardous environment his most precious organ, the representative
of his pleasure-ego; he can therefore quite easily permit himself
the luxury of erection, since in consequence of the identification
which has taken place the carefully guarded member certainly will
not get lost, seeing that it remains with a being with whom the ego
has identified itself. Thus there is brought about in the act of
coitus a successful compromise between the desire to give out and
the desire to retain, between an egotistic and a libidinal striving.

(*Thalassa*, p. 17)

Of course, in this case, the amphimictic foreplay is modelled
on a very limited phallocentric notion of heterosexuality.
Ferenczi is naturally cautious and ambivalent about the status of other amphimictic forms of foreplay, such as cunnilingus, sodomy or fellatio, given that these were formally desig-
nated as criminal activities at the time. None the less, it is
implicit in the amphimixis formula of transference play that
foreplay is pluralistic; it fuses eroticisms derived from both
the primordial mother and father lines of transference. Much
amphimictic foreplay ritual may therefore displace homosexual or narcissistic drives, even though they are formally
directed towards a heterosexual object choice. Similarly, any
amphimictic form, even coprophilia, becomes viewed as 'perversion' only when it is mediated by guilt or the 'language of
passion' (1, pp. 328ff.; see pp. 85, 197).

* * *

A major problem with the amphimixis model is its implicit syncretism: no matter how different or separate the erotic constellations involved, amphimixis will supposedly be able to create a common site in which drive and object relate. This may demand numerous displacements through determined symbolic registers, following the set oedipal progression from oral, anal, phallic to genital, yet it will still produce an effect that derives from this difference and separation. One could well imagine that any psychoanalyst trying to stem this kind of range and possible contradiction in a theoretical manner would opt for an abstraction that would remove problems of detailed psychological description to the level of primary process; Bion's alpha function springs to mind here.[11] Ferenczi, however, is never prone to this method of argument or description. Instead, he chooses to define this syncretic function of amphimixis by a term which could not be more concrete, namely *character*: 'we have to ascribe to the constitution of the admixture and to the finer or grosser apportionment of the ingredients of this combination of erotisms,' he explains, 'an enormous importance as regards not only genital normality or individuality but character formation in particular, which latter. . .is to be regarded as in large measure the psychic superstructure and the psychic transcript of these erotisms' (*Thalassa*, p. 12). In the context of 1920s psychoanalytic debate, this choice of term could not be more controversial. Karl Abraham and then Wilhelm Reich stress how 'character' stems from the no-man's land between sensorial/emotional affect and the exterior world (Abraham, 1919; Reich, 1925, 1929, 1933). Reich highlights this 'no-man's land' by defining 'character' somatically in terms of 'armouring', or the unconscious muscular tension which determines body posture. (The German word for this, 'Panzierung', derives from 'Panzer', or an 'armoured tank'). 'Character' obviously has to defend itself from some heavy external aggression.

Perhaps the heaviest form of external aggression that any character has to defend against is sexual abuse. It is often assumed that the thicker the 'armour' the character has developed, the less likely it is that the assault will break through to the creative amphimictic process; in adults, the whole symbolic network of language will supposedly be more able to defuse the shock and consciously absorb it as 'experience'.[12] In children, however, it is assumed that the creative process and symbolic network will be less secure, so that the 'character' as a whole may be smashed. Karl Abraham, for example, believes that child sex abuse is a major cause of psychosis ('On the significance of sexual trauma in childhood for the symptomatology of dementia praecox' [1907] 1955, pp. 13–20).

The problem with many views of child sexual abuse is that they totally ignore the input of the abused. They either deny the existence of infantile sexuality or question its value and integrity. So the abuser's desire is seen either to scour the surface of a tabula rasa or to render the infantile character's 'experience' inappropriate or useless. Such attitudes inflict a more surreptitious form of abuse, because they ignore the way in which the child experiences such events. They take it that 'shock' is totally exterior to character, so does not impinge on the erotic registers that normally fuse amphimictically to produce transferences somewhere between 'love' and 'hate'. The shock just switches off the symbolic system of displacements altogether. The children either experience permanent amnesia or are *better off* just forgetting what happened. This attitude is particularly noxious in a certain form of 'disclosure' interview, where the interviewers are often uniquely concerned to establish sufficient legal evidence to convict the abuser, rather than to care for the person who has actually experienced this abuse.[13] The guilty is accused and punished, and the innocent is sent into 'care' and left unattended with a whole range of unexplored ambivalences relating to 'guilt', usually for destroying someone or breaking up a family.

My point in raising such views here is that they are often erroneously associated with Ferenczi. Foremost in promoting this *mésalliance* is Jeffrey Masson, who attributes to Ferenczi sudden *ante-mortem* clairvoyance that child sexual abuse is the prime cause of adult neurosis. Freud – as Masson reminds us – had originally discovered this, but 'assaulted the truth' to support his own ambition and defend against his own childhood 'abuse' (Masson, 1984). Ferenczi's 'rediscovery', therefore, activated the worst Freudian anger. Ferenczi was rebuffed and his theories censored. None the less – Masson suggests – we should not be too quick to hand out sympathy and medals to Ferenczi. He 'never dared' tell Freud this 'truth' in its entirety nor even take this revelatory line of thought to its conclusion (Masson, 1984, pp. 147, 166), namely, that 'there is something in the very nature of engaging in therapy that leads to abuse' or that therapy reproduces the structure of child sex abuse (Masson, 1989, p. 166). Furthermore, to add insult to injury, Masson feels the need to put Ferenczi in his 'rightful place': 'I should make it clear that, although I regard Ferenczi's ideas as a move in the right direction, I still feel he remained a "therapist", somebody who wished to impose his own views of the world on somebody else' (ibid., p. 115).

Masson's views of Ferenczi are misguided in four major ways. First, neither Ferenczi nor Freud, nor indeed the whole psychoanalytic movement, 'assaulted the truth' of child sexual abuse. Views of sexual abuse changed, certainly, but only in so far as the child's perception and containment of trauma were concerned. Absolutely crucial in such theoretical transformations were Freud's 'My views on the part played by sexuality in the aetiology of the neuroses' (1906, 7, pp. 271ff.) and Abraham's 'The experiencing of sexual traumas as a form of sexual activity' ([1907] 1968, pp. 47ff.). These papers stated that children, as individuals, were involved in abusive incidents in different ways and should be respected and supported in their individual responses to these trauma. Crucial in this was the role of their 'fantasy' in accommodating incestuous desire within the set family structure.

Second, Masson totally misses the legal context in which Ferenczi and psychoanalysts in general had to situate their views of child sexual abuse. In many countries, the sentence for raping a child was death. For this reason, medical specialists in the field urged diagnostic caution and insisted on incontrovertible physical evidence rather than simple acceptance of a child's testimony. Brouardel, one of Masson's sources, actually took a strong and rather reactionary view on this: 'One speaks often of the candour of children. Nothing is more false. Their imagination likes to create stories in which they are the heroes' (1883, p. 8). Ambroise Tardieu, another of Masson's sources, went even further, and suggested that all sexual crimes – and he included homosexuality among these – indicated degeneracy, so were incurable, and best punished by death (1852–4). In this context, the purported psychoanalytic 'assault on truth' was unfounded. If nothing else, such 'truth' was rendered problematic by the criminal context. One of the strengths of the psychoanalytic model was that it refused the criminal and punishment models, and proposed instead a psycho-sexual model for understanding and caring for all those involved.

Third, it is absurd to suggest that Ferenczi actually 'discovered the truth' of child sex abuse only at the end of his life (Masson, 1984, pp. 161ff.). It is true that he came to the conclusion that child rape was more common than he had previously thought (3, p. 161). It is also true that some of his 'mutual analyses', notably with Elizabeth Severn, reactivated memories of sexual abuse he himself had suffered as a child. The following account indicates the nature of such re-activation.

> I submerged myself deeply in the reproduction of infantile experiences; the most evocative image was the vague appearance of female figures, probably servant girls from earliest childhood; then the image of a corpse, whose abdomen I was opening up, presumably in the dissecting room; linked to this the mad fatnasy that I was being pressed into this wound in the corpse. Interpretation: the after-effect [*Nachträglichkeit*] of passionate scenes, which presumably did take place, in the course of which a housemaid probably allowed me to play with her breasts, but then pressed my head between her legs, so I became frightened and felt I was suffocating. This is the source of my hatred of females: I want to dissect them for it, that is, to kill them. This is why my mother's accusation 'You are my murderer' cut to the heart and led to (1) a compulsive desire to help anyone who is suffering, especially women; and (2) a flight from situations in which I would have to be aggressive. Thus inwardly the feeling that in fact I am a good chap, also exaggerated reactions of rage, even at trivial affronts, and finally exaggerated reactions of guilt at the slightest lapse.
>
> (*Diary*, 17 March 1932, pp. 60-1)

It is quite clear that the 'accuracy' of the recollection of sexual abuse is not the main concern here. At best, details are 'probably' correct, and scenes 'presumably' did take place. It is also evident that there is not one 'scene' involved, but many. They are not related in sequence, but through 'deferred action', that is, they mutually influence each other; the mother's accusation, for example, reflects back on the dissection episode, which in turn relates to the incident of suffocation between the housemaid's legs. Fantasy also plays a formative role here, not just in the 'mad fantasy' of being pressed into the wound, but also in generating the vagueness and uncertainty of the dissecting room and seduction scenes. Furthermore, he is not the passive recipient of 'abuse' but, on the contrary, initiates it; he is 'allowed' to play with the housemaid's breasts, but then she responds in a way that he fails to understand, which indeed deeply frightens him. The 'abuse' therefore represents a 'confusion' (*Sprachverwirrung*) of the languages of tenderness and passion, and not rape.

This is not a new 'discovery' for Ferenczi. Throughout his career, he reflected on the nature of sexual abuse, not least in his own autobiographical context. This is most evident in his correspondence with Freud. In one letter, for example, he links the dream of a black cat that jumps on him, to phallic rivalry with his brother Karl, to hatred for his mother who was strong (in contrast to the 'weak' father whom he loved), and finally to the following 'seduction' scene:

> I envied the bravery of a young (though one year older) schoolfriend: his penis was bigger, 'beautifully brown', and had blue veins. As I was about 5 years old, he seduced me [*verleite er mich*] to allow him to stick his penis in my mouth. I remember the feeling of disgust that surged up in me (I feared he might have urinated in my mouth). I would not let him do it a second time.
>
> (Ferenczi to Freud, 26 December 1912)

Again, the central 'problem' here is the confusion of the languages of tenderness and passion. He is not the passive victim of 'abuse', but *amphimixes* desire, rivalry and envy, as well as their oral, anal and genital components.

This leads me to the fourth, and final, misrepresentation Masson imposes on Ferenczi, namely the conflation of 'seduction' and 'rape'. Such conflation is not unique to Masson; indeed it is now common to group all psychoanalytic work on child sex abuse under the label of the 'seduction theory'. In fact, Ferenczi, like Freud, stresses the variety of types of child sexual abuse. At one extreme, there is the rape (*Vergewaltigung*) of children. At the other, there is erotic play with children, in which the child may actively participate, or even be initiatory, but which may never reach actual penetration; this is the seduction (*Verführung* or *Verleitung*) of children.[14] The main confusion that results from ignoring this distinction is the suggestion that analysts subvert the reality of 'rape' by calling it 'seduction'. Alice Miller, for example, claims that 'the word "seduction" reinforces the wishful thinking of the adult, who assumes that the child shares his or her desires; these projections are absent from the word "abuse"' (1985, p. 129). In short, like Masson, she argues that the use of the term 'seduction' by analysts simply compacts the original abuse. In her terms, 'infantile sexuality' in general is a psychoanalytic wish fulfillment that conceals the reality of rape ('Is there such a thing as infantile sexuality?', 1985, pp. 121ff.).

This bears no relation whatsoever to the original texts under discussion. Take the prototype from Masson's supposed 'proof' of Ferenczi's last 'revelation', the famous 'last' text, 'Confusion of tongues between adults and the child' (1933). 'A typical way', Ferenczi writes,

> in which incestuous seductions (*Verführungen*) may occur is this: an adult and a child love each other, the child nursing the

playful fantasy of taking the role of mother to the adult. This play may assume erotic forms but remains, nevertheless, on the level of tenderness. It is not so, however, with pathological adults, especially if they have been disturbed in their balance and self-control by some misfortune or by the use of intoxicating drugs. They mistake the play of children for the desires of a sexually mature person or even allow themselves – irrespective of any consequences – to be carried away. The real rape [*Tatsächliche Vergewaltigung*] of girls who have hardly grown out of the age of infants, similar sexual acts of mature women with boys, and also enforced homosexual acts, are more frequent occurrences than has hitherto been assumed.

(3, pp. 161–2; cf. *Bausteine*, 3, p. 518)

There are a number of clear distinctions evident in this quote: first of all Ferenczi's own 'languages of tenderness and passion', which, as we have seen, are far from unilinear or reductive to a supposed simple 'reality'; second, the distinction between the 'normal' and the 'pathological', suggesting that drugs might mediate between the two in some circumstances; third, the distinction between 'seduction' that can begin 'on the level of tenderness', even incorporating 'love between an adult and a child', and 'real rape', which is shocking and brutal; and, finally, the distinction of various sexual orientations, and the relative position of men and women within them. None of these distinctions are recognized if 'seduction' is imposed as a blanket term for the 'abuse' that adults, and, by adumbration, analysts, impose on 'innocent' children.[15]

* * *

The great strength in Ferenczi's views of child sex abuse derives from the refusal to reduce complex associated issues to a simple 'reality'. Even the seemingly simple notion of the languages of tenderness and of passion conceals, in fact, great subtlety and diversity. As with every language, it would be naive to believe that the words that articulate tenderness and passion actually encapsulate the 'reality' of the objects they denote. They play and amphimix along the tracks elaborated by transferences to those objects. In the first place, they displace symbolically; they approximate to the primordial fantasy scenarios and shift across the prescribed oedipal registers of desire and hate. They both therefore have the capacity to contain considerable ambivalence. The language of tenderness in adults, for example, can carry unconscious infantile incestuous desire; in children, the same language can incorporate elements of genital passion. The analyst must be sensitive to these nuances, and refuse to allow inter- pretative preconception to foreclose the power of the ambiv- alence. Ferenczi summarizes this as follows: 'a deep signifi- cance must . . . be attached to the *repressed incestuous affections of adults, which masquerade as tenderness*. On the other hand, I am bound to confess that children themselves manifest a readiness to engage in genital eroticism more vehemently and far earlier than we used to suppose' (original italics, 3, p. 121).

Ferenczi's model also refuses to be predisposed to view adults' accounts of their own sexual abuse as *either* 'real' *or* the product of 'unconscious fantasy'. Like Freud, he is well aware that such accounts can combine both elements in complex ways, following the dynamics of 'deferred action'. Ferenczi's approach to the relative importance of 'uncon- scious fantasy' here is inspired by his view of the destructive dimension of play. Like Klein – but some ten years before her – he maintains that primal destructive drives (*trieben*) play through the dual structures of projection and introjection. Similarly, he believes that the ego paradoxically accretes around the introjective aspect of this destruction. 'The remarkable thing', he explains, 'about this self-destruction is that here (in adaption, in the recognition of the surrounding world, in the forming of objective judgements) destruction does indeed become the "cause of being" [*Spielrein*]. A partial destruction of the ego is tolerated, but only for the purpose of constructing out of what remains an ego of still greater resistance'[16] (2, p. 377).

Ferenczi believes that such introjected destructive drives can be reactivated and reverberate within children's experience of sex abuse. They may not just be 'shocked' by the imposition of violence, but may identify with it and even introject the adult's guilt feelings. In fact, it is often this violent 'superimposition' (*Auflegen*) on the child's erotic amphimixis that gives specific form to the primordial fantasy scenarios; that is, renders them complex, or ambivalent and, accordingly, through deferred action, transforms the 'trauma' into a diffuse network of feeling. In the case of violent rape (*Vergewaltigung*), the child often retreats entirely into unconscious fantasy and splits or forecloses the external world; 'the attack as a rigid external reality ceases to exist and in a traumatic trance the child succeeds in maintaining the previous situation of tenderness' (3, p. 162). In cases of seduction (*Verführungen*), the articulation between the languages of tenderness is more 'confused' (Ferenczi uses the word '*verwirren*', which also means entangled).

It is hatred that traumatically surprises and frightens the child while being loved by the adult, that changes him from a spontaneously and innocently playing being into a guilty love-automaton imitating the adult anxiously and self-effacingly. Their own guilt feelings and the hatred felt towards the seductive child-partner fashion the love relation of the adults into a frightening struggle (primal scene) for the child. For the adult, this ends in the moment of orgasm, while infantile sexuality – in the absence of the 'struggle of the sexes' – remains at the level of forepleasure and knows gratifications only in the sense of 'saturation' and not the feelings of annihilation of orgasm.

(3, p. 167)

What is most revolutionary in this approach – and, sadly, most misunderstood – is the total respect for what the child makes of a catastrophic situation. Ferenczi has no time for 'moral superiority' that punishes guilty adults and gives neither thought nor support to the child's means of coming to terms with such experience. It is easy to assume that the child either has no sexuality or that such experience will have no impact on its 'adult' experience of life; but this betrays the very nature of the child's affective bond with the world and denies its right to negotiate its own way through its tragedies, as well as its joys. It shuts down the language of tenderness and imprisons all reasons for pain in the adult language of passion. In short, the children who are deprived of a space to relate to abuse in their own terms often come to find the right voice as patients in psychoanalysis. Above all, then, the analyst must seek out and nourish the language of tenderness. The foreplay for this is easy enough: to remove the block, allow the language of passion to illustrate that adults are often 'dangerous fools, to whom one cannot tell the truth without the risk of being punished' (1, p. 204).

Chapter 4

Coitus

Mutual attraction is nothing but the expression of the fantasy of veritably merging oneself with the body of the partner or perhaps of forcing one's way in toto *into it (as a substitute for the mother's womb); the ultimate sexual union is only the partial realization of this purpose.*

—Sándor Ferenczi, 1922, *Thalassa*, p. 34

PSYCHOANALYSTS OFTEN PREACH grim sermons about sexual intercourse. They talk of the deceptions surrounding and subverting the act. Even its supposedly more *playful* aspects are supposed to articulate desires for return to the breast or womb, or for repair to the damage inflicted in the primal castration scenario (Lacan, 1977, pp. 9–18). Lovers' little rituals, for example, such as mock fights, jokes, obscene word or baby-talk routines, are all supposed to form along prescribed lines of primal fantasy and play through the 'binary' logic of the presence/absence (fort-da) game (Derrida, 1980, pp. 315ff.; Laplanche, 1989, pp. 36–7). Such analysts give little or no indication, therefore, of lasting joyful release or creative expression through coitus.[17] Instead, they present only an endless compulsion to repeat a doomed act.

To some extent, Ferenczi supports this view: 'The act of coitus. . .', he says, 'is reminiscent of those melodramas in which, while there are of course dark clouds threatening all kinds of destruction, just as in a real tragedy, there is always the feeling that "everything will turn out all right"' (*Thalassa*,

p. 42). He also gives some credence to the 'primal scene' structure of the act.

> The tension which during coitus keeps the participants in a kind of suspense is in itself unpleasurable, and only the expectation of its prospective relief makes it at the same time pleasurable. This kind of unpleasurable tension has a good deal of similarity to anxiety, which, as we know from Freud, is always a reproduction of the unpleasurable sensations connected with the shock attending the process of being born.
>
> (*Thalassa*, p. 34)

Ferenczi, however, does not confine all these dark clouds, suspense and tension to an early metaphorical playpen in which we all become fixed in our ways of playing with the gaps in experience. On the contrary, he views coitus as presenting a unique opportunity to escape such infantile fixations and broaden the quality and range of experience. It is therefore social convention, transmitted and reinforced by sex education, that leads people to miss this opportunity and remain bound to the anxiety of early infancy. This is particularly evident in common sexual difficulties that disturb or even prevent coitus. Many men, for example, suffer from a 'small penis complex', which has a psychological rather than a physiological basis. The growth of their penis may be 'normal', but their idea of it remains infantile; they are still caught within the fantasy of copulation with mother, whose vagina seems much too big for them (Ferenczi, 1, p. 145; *Diary*, p. 164). Women who view their lover's penis as too small may well also be reflecting the infantile idea of their father's penis; conversely, their fear that their vagina is too small or will get torn often relates to a similar source. Indeed, Ferenczi observes, this infantile perspective seems remarkably well fixed behind Western supposed erotic 'norms', hence the general appeal, power and often threat that very large breasts and penises exert in popular consciousness (1, p. 147). Psychoanalysis can thus perform a vital social function by revealing the infantile structure of such complexes. It can stem the obsessional repetition of primal fear and anxiety, and promote instead more fluidity and freedom of sexual expression.

Ferenczi maintains that one of the critical tasks of psychoanalytic sex education is to explain how the body–mind relationship functions in coitus. It is one thing to argue for a 'persistence' of infantile psychic structures, but quite another to elaborate the mix of pleasure/pain or tension/release in copulating bodies. 'Transference' and 'displacement', he argues, do not remain locked up in a particularly abstract space in the head, but 'innervate' (*nervenkraft zuführen*) the nervous and muscular systems of the body (2, pp. 230–1). This is proved superficially by observing the effect of thought on the body. When most people think, the general tonus of their musculature is increased. Some more inhibited types, however, have to stop walking to think; more motor-active types have to walk to slow down the rapidity of their thoughts. Likewise, masturbation 'innervates' in different ways in different people. It follows different rhythms and evokes distinct sequences of body sensation. It is also displaced to various body locations: 'larval', or 'infantile', masturbation, for example, often involves frequent clonic quivers of the calf muscles or rhythmically crossing, pressing or banging the legs together; this can be further displaced and expressed through ritual nose- or ear-boring or fiddling with nails, hair or beard (2, p. 195).[18] Finally, at a deeper organic level, the sphincters in the throat, intestine and genitals convey specific erotic innervations; in hysterical cases, coital dysfunction is frequently displaced to the larynx or to the bowels; men sometimes lose the capacity to ejaculate and women cease to menstruate (2, pp. 268ff.).

The location, shape and rhythm of these different innervations do not disappear in coitus but rather contribute to its dynamic form. Coitus therefore combines or 'amphimixes' various levels of erotic play, including masturbatory rituals, which spread in various ways through the nervous, muscle and sphincter systems. Societies variously limit this amphimixis, judging fellatio, sodomy or cunnilingus, for example, as criminal perversions (cf. Hirschfeld, 1959, pp. 425ff.). Ferenczi regards such interdictions as an inadequate defence against general regressive psychic trends (*Zugen*). Even if such 'perversions' are not actually performed during coitus, they may be symbolically displaced and reappear elsewhere. Obscene language, for example, invokes and exploits the whole perverse range, not least copro- and uro-lagnia (the sexual use of faeces and urine), which may not be permitted to oneself but are certainly fit for adversaries (1, pp. 136–8). Even the politest, most socially adept person, Ferenczi contends, will produce a surprising array of obscenities when shocked (1, p. 151; cf. 2, p. 227).

Another common social outlet for banned eroticisms is graffiti. Ferenczi notes that these often displace exhibitionist drives and reflect an infantile mix of desire and anxiety concerning the body's erotic sites (1, pp. 105ff; cf. Freud, 1905a). This explains the frequent exaggerated depiction of male and female genitals, as well as earlier depictions of female pubic and axillary hair, which was excised both from the 'Greek aesthetic ideal' and general public display (*Thalassa*, p. 38; cf. Irigaray, 1974). Moreover, graffiti are often located either in public toilets, ideal copro- or uro-lagnic sites, or on the most grandiose or 'authoritative' walls and buildings in town. Ferenczi and Freud were particularly struck by examples of the latter while strolling in Central Park in New York in 1909; even in 'such a prudish country as America', Ferenczi noted, there were 'chalk drawings and inscriptions on a beautiful marble flight of stairs' (1, p. 144).

Ferenczi claims that one of the most repressed eroticisms at play in coitus is the homoerotic.

> A part of unsatisfied homoeroticism remains 'free-floating' and demands to be appeased; since this is impossible under the conditions of present-day civilization, this quantity of sexual hunger has to undergo a displacement, namely, on to the feeling-relationship to the opposite sex. I quite seriously believe that the men of today are one and all obsessively heterosexual as the result of this affective displacement; in order to free themselves from men, they become the slaves of women.
>
> (1, p. 316)

Men therefore tend to idealize women as 'homoerotic objects', that is, to view them as sexually passive recipients of phallic penetration (1, p. 301). Of course, this totally ignores the amphimixic range of female sexuality, much (if not all) of which is independent of phallic eroticism. Men therefore further displace their homoerotic anxiety by identification with the 'Don Juan' type, which, contrary to popular belief, often represents obsessional homo- rather than hetero-sexuality: Don Juans tend to worship their own phallic prowess in the 'conquest' of numerous women (1, p. 316; cf. Rank, 1975). Unconsciously, it is not the women's approbation which is sought, but rather that of other men, who will either rival with further phallic display (i.e. 'active' or 'subject' homoeroticism) or concede admiringly (i.e. 'passive' or 'object' homoeroticism).

Ferenczi's analysis of coitus is unusual, particularly in its historical context, if only because he refuses to pay homage to a supposed 'normal stereotypic event', which somehow embodies 'genital maturity'. Indeed, he dismisses the whole notion of 'genital maturity' as a reductive and positively dangerous myth, which imposes even more repression on socially intimidated individuals. It is neither wise nor necessary to restrict the range of eroticisms at play in coitus, unless there is some palpable harm inflicted on one or more partners. There is no essential reason, for example, why adults should feel guilty for masturbating or committing sodomy, fellatio and cunnilingus. They are rendered 'guilty' only within the terms of the classic oedipal development scheme, in which phallic or anal eroticism is 'regressive', hence subversive of 'genital', or 'objective', recognition of the family order. It is only the oedipal 'language of passion' that forces guilt and rigidity into the essential free play of the 'language of tenderness'.

In this respect, Ferenczi is not content simply to state that considerable ignorance surrounds the aetiology of 'perverse sexual acts'. Rather, he chooses to campaign publicly for the reform of laws that advocate punishment for such practices. As early as 1902, for example, in the 'Rosa K. Case', he argues that transvestites should be allowed to walk the streets untrammelled (Lorin, 1983, pp. 199ff.). Similarly, in 1907, he becomes a vocal member of Magnus Hirschfeld's *Wissenschaftlich-humanitäres Komitee* which campaigns to change the law that punishes homosexuality as a criminal offence. (At the same time, Freud, in contrast, keeps well clear of the WHK [letter to Jung, 25 February 1908]). None the less, Ferenczi underscores this activism with tolerance rather than a genuine sense of equality. 'Perverse sexual acts' are always seen as paranoid defences against the demands of heterosexuality (cf. 'On the part played by homosexuality in the pathogenesis of paranoia', 1912, 1, pp. 154ff.). He reaffirms this view at the end of his life, in a *Diary* entry entitled 'Perversions are not fixations but the products of fear': 'Anxiety, fear in the face of normality (trauma) provoke flight to deviant ways to satisfy desire. Homosexuality (autosadism) is forbidden, yet not so "impossible", "unmentionable", "unthinkable" as heterosexual union' (p. 172). Homosexuals, therefore, demand the greatest sensitivity in analysis to overcome their paranoid distrust, and hence to stem to some extent their flight from heterosexual eroticism. Not that Ferenczi ever claims to 'cure', that is, permanently remove, the homoerotic; he simply wishes, perhaps naively, to prevent paranoid exclusion of the heteroerotic.

Of course, according to Ferenczi, these coital amphimixes are symbolically incorporated in the analytical situation. The transference is structured around the particular erotic combinations that analysand and analyst bring to the analysis. The progression of the transference also mirrors the peculiar rhythms and rituals of coitus. This can be seen in many ways, but perhaps most importantly in the erotic 'innervation' of the patient's body. Patients, for example, periodically engage in 'larval' masturbation during analysis; they press their legs together or tense their muscles (2, p. 191). The homoerotic is indicated non-verbally by the patient turning on the couch, often full on to the face (2, p. 242). On the verbal level, the amphimixic shape takes much longer to emerge.

> The general attitude of the participants during the sex act itself, the emotions which they manifest during it, have received the least consideration up to the present. As if with regard to these affects human beings would guard their deepest secrets, a well-nigh insuperable feeling of shame prevents them from giving information about them. Even in analysis, where analysands have to communicate all their reactions, they learn only at long

last and only if necessary to describe their subjective train of experiences in the sex act, long after they have become accustomed to stating its objective events without reservation.

(*Thalassa*, p. 33)

* * *

Freud comments that 'the spheres of sexuality and obscenity offer the amplest occasions for obtaining comic pleasure alongside pleasurable sexual excitement; for they can show human beings in their dependence on bodily needs (degradation) or they can reveal the physical demands lying behind the claim of mental love (unmasking)' (Freud, 1905b, p. 286). This assumes that 'the claim of mental love' is fragile and vulnerable, and is constantly undermined by 'bodily needs'. Rarely do love and sex combine, and, even then, 'the physical demands' behind coitus threaten to plunge the relationship into the obscene. 'Smut' often intervenes (as in English, the German '*Schmutz*' also connotes dirt and smudges). Someone usually gets 'dirty', and someone else feels 'degraded'. Obscene jokes trace out this 'unmasking' process (cf. Freud, 1905b, pp. 140ff.).

In the post-Freudian era, biographers face great difficulties in accounting for their subjects' attempts to reconcile 'the claim of mental love' and 'bodily needs'. On the one hand, they feel obliged to enter bedrooms and recount intimate details; on the other hand, often what they find is either pathetic or shocking and seems to degrade their subject. This is particularly the case with biographies of psychoanalysts themselves. It is extra pathetic or shocking to find out that analysts do not just *witness* the configurations of the 'sexual aetiology of the neuroses' on the couch, but also add a few special twists on their own behalf. It is confounding to learn, for example, that Jung, a great critic of the 'sexual aetiology of the neuroses', actually had a long and active, adulterous sex life; an aspect strangely absent from his published autobiography, though apparently not from the original manuscript (Carotenuto, 1982). Different, but equally disturbing, erotic 'tensions' have emerged in recent biographies of Anna Freud, Karen Horney and Melanie Klein (Young-Bruehl, 1988; Quinn, 1988; Grosskurth, 1985).[19] Obviously, psychoanalysis promotes this form of critical study of 'ideas' in the context of 'bodily needs' and 'physical demands'; funnily enough, this may not just 'degrade' the subject, but can also render their 'ideas' human in their vulnerability, even prompting the odd smile – it can 'nourish and lighten' what otherwise would be a heavy and unpalatable set of ingredients (cf. 'Ferenczi fritters', in Hillman and Boer, 1985, pp. 138–40).

In Ferenczi's case, biographical excursions into his intimate sex life have been decidedly heavy and destructive, rather than warmly illustrative of the frailty and vulnerability of 'mental love'. Among the many charges made against him are that he engaged in sexual relations with his patients and finally totally lost control of the analytical situation when he lapsed into a brief reactive psychosis at the end of his life (Jones, 3, p. 165). Since more documentary evidence has become available, it is clear that these charges rest principally on an exchange of letters between Freud and Ferenczi, in which Freud states that 'according to my recollection, a tendency to sexual play with patients was not completely alien to you in preanalytic times, so that the new technique [mutual analysis] could be linked to an old error. That is why I spoke in my last letter of a new puberty' (13 December 1931). To this, Ferenczi replies: 'Your fear that I might develop into a second Stekel [who reputedly had sex with patients] is, I believe, unfounded. "Sins of youth", mistakes, once they have been overcome and analytically worked through, can even make one wiser and more prudent than people who have never experienced such storms' (27 December 1931). In short, Freud had heard from a patient, Clara Thompson, that she was 'allowed to kiss Papa Ferenczi as often as I like', and therefore assumed that Ferenczi had returned to 'old errors' from 'preanalytic times'. Critics now generally assume that this exchange of letters vindicates Ferenczi (Torok, 1984; Masson, 1984, 1989; Dupont, 1988).

What is left unexplained, however, is the reference to the 'sins of youth' and 'sexual play with patients. . .in preanalytic times'. It is not generally known that this refers principally to Ferenczi's major life crisis which began in 1911, and is 'preanalytic' in so far as it antedates his analysis with Freud by three years (cf. Sabourin, 1985, pp. 57–8). In many ways, this is reminiscent of that 'melodrama' which Ferenczi associates with coitus: 'While there are of course dark clouds threatening all kinds of destruction, just as in a real tragedy, there is always the feeling that "everything will turn out all right"' (see p. 117). To recap the main story-line: in July 1911, Ferenczi agrees to take his lover Gizella's daughter, Elma, into analysis for depression. He loses control of the transference situation, ceases to desire Gizella and predictably fantasizes erotically about Elma (letter to Freud, 14 November 1911). His correspondence with Freud details these sexual agonies, notably his intermittent impotence, as well as the joys of assuaging his 'coital hunger'. There is also a lengthy and moving account of his attempt to balance the deep 'mental love' for Gizella with the wild sexual desires for Elma, all the time fearing he will cause an irreparable rift between them, and also possibly cause Elma's suicide (letter to Freud, 3 December 1911).

Ferenczi's initial response is to consider marriage to Elma; he talks, in fact, of *'fantasies* of marriage' (14 November 1911). Freud takes Elma into analysis in January 1912, and advises Ferenczi against this course of action; after fourteen days of consultation, he says she is too infantile for marriage (letter to Ferenczi, 23 January 1912). Ferenczi should look rather to his 'mental love' for Gizella. Later that year, Elma departs for the United States, soon becomes engaged to an American, Laurvick, and eventually marries him. Ferenczi is obviously deeply distressed by this. He suffers from stomach and intestinal pains, as well as bouts of intense fatigue. He enters into three weeks' analysis with Freud in July 1914, but this is interrupted by the mobilization of Austro-Hungarian troops prior to the outbreak of the First World War. Ferenczi achieves enough clarity to decide to propose to Gizella only in spring 1917, while convalescing after an attack of stomach bleeding. Significantly, he is afraid of rejection and asks Freud to act as his intermediary (letter to Freud, 24 March 1917). Gizella accepts and prepares her husband, Géza Pálos, for divorce. On 1 March 1919, however, on arrival at the town hall for their wedding ceremony, they are told that her husband has just died of a heart attack. Ferenczi sees this as an ill omen. According to one source, he never manages fully to renounce his wish to marry Elma (Ferenczi and Groddeck, p. 135).

There are two important features of this 'melodrama' that distinguish it from a simple case of sex with a patient. First, the erotic amphimixis involves not two, but three participants. This particular *ménage à trois* is further oedipally complicated by the fact that the two women involved are mother and daughter. Furthermore, the situation is adulterous, in a close family and community network dating back to childhood. Indeed, Gizella's other daughter, Magda, later marries Ferenczi's younger brother, Lajos. In this context, therefore, containment of the extent of emotional repercussions is difficult if not impossible.

Second, the erotic outcome is heavily influenced, if not determined, by Freud, who initially agrees to take Elma into analysis and advises both Gizella and Ferenczi. Freud conflates his role of confidant with that of both father and analyst. He suddenly stops calling Ferenczi 'Dear Friend', and uses 'Dear Son' instead, arguing that he must adopt such a fatherly role when someone lets their complexes create so much difficulty for them (letter to Ferenczi, 17 November 1911). This contrasts quite markedly with the attitude Freud took earlier when Jung confessed his affair with a patient, Sabina Spielrein: 'Such experiences', Freud had written to Jung,

> though painful, are necessary and hard to avoid. Without them we cannot really know life and what we are dealing with . . .They help us to develop the thick skin we need and to dominate 'counter-transference', which is after all a permanent problem for us; they teach us to displace our own affects to best advantage. They are a 'blessing in disguise'.
>
> (7 June 1909, Freud and Jung, 1974, pp. 230–1)

Indeed, Freud refuses to accept Ferenczi's basic 'bodily need' for Elma, but suggests a deeper oedipal dynamic. He writes immediately to Gizella to attribute the situation to Ferenczi's 'domineering homosexuality' which is projected on to her child (Elma), so that Ferenczi can take revenge (*Rache*) on his own mother (letter to Gizella Pálos, 17 December 1911). To some extent, this mirrors Ferenczi's account to Freud of both his oedipal situation – loving his mild father and hating his fierce mother – and his early homoerotic experiences (cf. letter to Freud, 26 December 1912). Freud clearly feels that Gizella can help Ferenczi come to terms with these, but as a 'mother', and at the expense of his erotic drives towards Elma (letter to Gizella, op. cit.).

However, 'masterly' this interpretation, it severely limits the erotic amphimixis which Ferenczi describes to Freud. It dismisses, for example, Ferenczi's desire to have children with Elma as 'infantile'. It also imposes the view that the homoerotic and heteroerotic are mutually exclusive. Now, within the analytic transference to Freud, Ferenczi accepts this and allows the interpretation to inform the development and outcome of his erotic life. But, as he comes later to analyse this transference, he uncovers precisely 'the thick skin' Freud developed 'to dominate the counter-transference' (following the comment to Jung on the Spielrein case): namely, that Freud himself had not analysed his own erotic input into this interpretation. Freud's own oedipal problems led him to support the mother to prevent the erotic free play of the son.

This particularly painful insight becomes increasingly prominent in Ferenczi's later relationship with Freud. He blames Freud's denial of countertransferential elements for commuting real erotic drives into convenient theories. 'The anxiety provoking idea,' Ferenczi writes,

> perhaps very strong in the unconscious, that the father must die when the son grows up, explains. . .[Freud's] fear of allowing any one of his sons to become independent. At the same time, it also shows us that Freud the son really did want to kill his father. Instead of admitting this, he founded the theory of the parricidal Oedipus, but obviously applied only to others, not to

himself. Hence the fear of allowing himself to be analysed, hence perhaps also the idea that in civilized adults primitive instinctual impulses are not real any more, that the oedipal disease is a childhood disease, like the measles.

(*Diary*, 4 August 1932, pp. 184–5)

An important amplification of this is that Freud's theory actually denies Ferenczi's own 'primitive instinctual impulses'. The theory side-tracks Ferenczi from questioning his own transference, and dependence on Freud, which further complicates the original 'melodrama', by evoking fear of attacking the adult to support the independence of the 'child' (namely the 'infantile tenderness' between himself and Elma). Moreover, the theory reinforces Ferenczi's collusion with Freud's own 'domineering homosexuality'. Why else would he either invite or allow Freud to arbitrate between the mother and daughter, or the adult and child? The only alternative is to divest Freud, and his theory, of the power to decide, in other words, symbolically to castrate the father and deprive the patriarchal metaphor of its discursive mastery. Of course, this is doubly difficult when the 'father' concerned holds a theory that renders aggression redundant. 'The mutually castration-directed aggressivity', Ferenczi explains, 'which in the unconscious is probably crassly aggressive, is overlaid by the need – which should be called homosexual – for a harmonious father–son relationship. In any case he [Freud] could, for example, tolerate my being a son only until the moment when I contradicted him for the first time' (*Diary*, 4 August 1932, pp. 184–5).

Crucial here is Ferenczi's belief that Freud assumes symbolic power through the transference to direct or even foreclose lines of sensual play within coitus. Freud's interpretation of Ferenczi's life crisis imposed boundaries between

supposed 'infantile' and 'adult' object choice, or between
Elma and Gizella, leaving Ferenczi 'free' henceforth to apply
these theoretical guidelines to defend a besieged frontier
control between the two. (Ironically, in German, the 'association' which is supposedly 'free' is sometimes rendered by the
word '*Einfall*', which means a 'collapse' or 'downfall', as well
as 'irruption' or 'sudden idea'.)[20] Furthermore, Ferenczi is
encouraged even more to defend these theoretical guidelines
in order to avoid Freud's own 'castration-directed aggressivity'. Once the theory fails, though, Ferenczi questions Freud's
own libidinal economy which produced the interpretation in
the first place. Why did Freud support Gizella against Elma?
'Freud', Ferenczi deduces,

> may have a personal aversion to the spontaneous female-orien-
> tated sexuality in women: idealization of the mother. He recoils
> from the task of having a sexually demanding mother, and
> having to satisfy her. At some point his mother's passionate
> nature may have presented him with such a task. (The primal
> scene may have rendered him relatively impotent.) *Castration of
> the father, the potent one, as a reaction to the humiliation he
> experienced, led to the construction of a theory in which the
> father castrates the son* and, moreover, is then revered by the son
> as a god. In his conduct Freud plays only the role of the
> castrating god, he wants to ignore the traumatic moment of his
> own castration in childhood; he is the only one who does not
> have to be analysed.
>
> (*Diary*, 4 August 1932, p. 188)

* * *

Once Ferenczi has established a parallel between the coital
erotic amphimixis and the erotic dynamic of transference

and countertransference, he begins to formulate his proposed reforms for psychoanalytic technique in terms of the oedipal constraints imposed on coitus. Particularly important here is the total exclusion of free-floating female sexuality in the transference and countertransference. By associating the analyst with the father, and imposing stern theoretical strictures, Freud 'castrates' the mother and refuses to allow her own eroticism any space. Not that Freud is alone in this. Patriarchal society generally imposes this symbolic castration on women from childhood. The problem is that mothers therefore also deprive children of this female erotic space. The analyst who attempts to occupy the female erotic must often then have to restore lost articulations of feeling. This parallels the role of the wife who has to open her husband to the female erotic in coitus.

> The right sort of wife will not imitate the boy's mother, who condemns sexuality altogether, not to mention incest; instead she will learn to reassure the inhibited boy of her love, whatever kinds of impulses he may feel, and even when he has given in to these impulses. As a reward for this self-denial she will witness an improvement in his self-esteem, the awakening of his sense of responsibility simultaneously with his potency, and thereby put an end to the compulsion to repeat that stems from his childhood. With the present trends in the education of women, such understanding and forgiving behaviour is hardly to be expected. . .The capacity for such adaptation to renunciation is perhaps explicable only if we assume the existence in nature of a second principle next to that of egoistical self-assertion, namely an appeasement principle; that is, selfishness (infantility, masculinity) versus motherliness, that is to say kindness.
>
> (*Diary*, 28 June 1932, p. 146)

Chapter 5

Love

The progress of the cure bears no relation to the depth of [*the patient's*] *theoretical insight, nor to the memories already laid bare.*

—Sándor Ferenczi, Address to The Hague Congress,
10 September 1920

Ferenczi consistently criticizes the overvaluation of theoretical insight in the analytical situation. First and foremost, he denounces analysts who pontificate in front of their patients. 'In real psychoanalysis', he warns, 'there is little room for moral or philosophical generalizations; it is an uninterrupted sequence of concrete experience [*Erlebnis*]' (2, p. 185). Indeed, patients respond extremely badly to such intellectualization: they 'do not react to theatrical phrases, but only to real sincere sympathy' (3, p. 161). This applies generally, even to patients who demand a broad intellectual framework in which to locate their experience. 'If we keep our cool, educational attitude, even vis-à-vis an opisthotonic patient [i.e. one whose body is tensed up with anxiety], we tear to shreds the last thread that connects him to us. The patient gone off into his trance is a *child indeed* who no longer reacts to intellectual explanations, only perhaps to maternal friendliness; without it, he feels lonely and abandoned in his greatest need' (3, p. 160).

In this context, moral or philosophical generalization can represent analysts' defence against their patients' transference and their own countertransference. They may fear that they will be sucked into their patients' erotic and emotional turmoil, and that their own intimate world will equally be implicated, so they assume a convenient distance through theory. Ferenczi maintains that no progress whatsoever is likely to be made in psychoanalysis unless such defence through distance is removed and the transference/counter-transference dynamic is allowed to take its course. A main objective of theoretical work in analysis might therefore be to facilitate this dynamic, particularly to remove strong, uncon-scious, countertransferential resistance. This is 'deconstruc-tive' (to use an appropriate contemporary term), because it aims to expose how analysts use a decontextualized body of psychoanalytic 'knowledge' to establish their own interpreta-tive 'power', rather than to appreciate the 'play' that under-lies the transference. Once this 'power' is removed, the ana-lyst will neither be defended by some immutable intellectual accuracy and superiority nor fixed to the father's primordial position in the transference, but instead capable of 'real sincere sympathy' or 'maternal friendliness'.

In this context, Ferenczi contends that arguments for the 'educative' role of the analyst are particularly deleterious. This has been quite an explosive issue throughout the history of the psychoanalytic movement, and has surfaced at most of the major 'crises', notably the Adler and Jung secessions, the 'Controversial Discussions' between the Anna Freud and Melanie Klein groups, and Jacques Lacan's expulsion from the IPA. It is rarely appreciated, however, that Ferenczi was crucial in rehearsing these arguments. Particularly formative was his passionate exchange on the subject with the Swedish analyst, Poul Bjerre, which took place at the Munich Con-gress in September 1913,[21] when the IPA was still in full crisis after Alfred Adler's resignation in April 1911.[22] Bjerre wished

to strengthen the authority, hence, in his view, the 'effective-
ness', of psychoanalytic treatment, by formally including the
patient's 'medical and ethical education' (Bjerre, 1911, 1914).
He defined this 'new authoritative analytical intervention' as
'clear spiritual guidance', which impressed many analysts at
the time, particularly Jung. 'Correcting Bjerre's paper gave
me an awful lot of work', Jung had earlier written to Freud,
'but it's a fine thing' (letter of 11 December 1911, Freud and
Jung, p. 470). Ferenczi strongly disagreed and denounced
such 'guidance' (*belehrung*) as 'interference' (*einmischung*),
as it differed little, in his opinion, from the imposition of
hypnotic suggestion. He also issued a 'special warning' that,
if generally accepted, such procedures would totally stifle
technical innovation in psychoanalysis (2, p. 235).

Superficially, Bjerre's position seemed to have many benefits. It was easy to request and judge a medical training. This
also provided useful social prestige and legal cover. Similarly, it seemed eminently sensible to direct patients to a
basic code of ethics, as, after all, they had to live and regain
their hold on a world which was supposedly thus codified. In
contrast, Ferenczi's demand for 'real sincere sympathy' and
'maternal friendliness' seemed far removed from academic
qualifications and could not easily be taught or examined.
Jung, for example, contended that this posed one of the main
obstacles to the general acceptability of psychoanalysis: 'psychological sensitivity. . .', he said, 'cannot be taken for
granted in every physician or psychologist' (1973, 2, p. 289).
Furthermore, the suggestion that transference should be allowed to play freely could be construed by the outside world
as encouraging patients to indulge their unethical, antisocial
drives. Analysts should therefore make it clear that they
wished to 'educate' the patient to 'give up' the negative aspects of transference; instead, the fostering of a uniquely

positive transference to the analyst would speed up the eventual 'cure' of the neurotic symptoms and facilitate the patient's re-integration into society (Bjerre, 1911, p. 342).

Ferenczi's characteristic response was to admit that his way might not conform to ruling scientific or social conventions, but at least it was true to psychoanalytic insight. There was a way to train psychoanalysts in 'real sincere sympathy' and 'maternal friendliness', and that was to insist that all trainee analysts undergo personal psychoanalysis themselves. It was up to analysts themselves to create their own appropriate 'social and scientific' environment for this, and not to expect other academic disciplines either to understand or to be supportive. Furthermore, it was important to observe that the whole notion of 'education' in modern Western societies had dangerous implications. Many patients actually came to analysts in the first place precisely because they had suffered deeply from such scientifically, socially or spiritually sanctioned 'guidance': 'the inordinate strictness in the punishment of sexual habits of childhood', Ferenczi explained, 'the systematic training of children to blind obedience and motiveless respect for their parents: all these are components of a method of education. . .that might also be called artificial breeding of neuropaths and sexually impotent people' (1, p. 32). Instead, therefore, patients expected something else from analysts, something that would nurture and perhaps heal them, even if it was not particularly socially respected or scientifically sanctioned. This 'something else' Ferenczi called 'love'.

The choice of the term 'love' was equally characteristic of Ferenczi. It was something to which most people aspired, but by which many felt cheated. Ferenczi went even further, and suggested that the wild desires and frustrations it aroused often drove people to psychotic breakdown. Even at the start of his career, before becoming a psychoanalyst, he defined it as a '"frontier zone" [*határterület*, in Hungarian, also means intermediate or borderline] between the pathological and the normal' ('*A szerelem a tudományban*', 'Love in the sciences', 1901; cf. Lorin, 1983, p. 156). Later, he added to the 'frontier' definition by drawing parallels between love and transference, which, as we have seen, also precariously negotiates fantasy and reality in erotic 'amphimixis'. Ferenczi stressed this parallel by frequently referring to 'transference-love' (*Übertragungs-Liebe*), rather than simple 'transference' (2, p. 290). An important effect of this was to render psychoanalytic work more difficult; hopefully, though, analysts would acquire critical skills that lovers often lack, thus assuaging pain and anxiety rather than causing it. 'Psychoanalytic "cure"', Ferenczi explained to Izette de Forest, 'is in direct proportion to the cherishing love given by the psychoanalyst to the patient; the love which the psychoneurotic patient *needs*, not necessarily the love which he thinks he needs and therefore demands' (de Forest, 1954, p. 15).

* * *

Unfortunately, there is an intractable problem with this use of the word 'love'. It suggests that the 'real sincere sympathy' and 'maternalistic friendliness' involved are anti-authoritarian or unpolluted by patriarchal authority. Mothers, or those who adopt them as a role model, may be relatively disadvantaged, even dependent, within the social or economic system, but their inner resources supposedly allow them to overcome this. In this formulation, they do not have to engage in much conscious activity, just follow their 'natural' inclinations and offer sincerity and tenderness as a mother offers milk to her infant.

To explore alternatives is not easy. To argue, for example, that a mother's natural inclinations are also structured within the socio-economic context, notably by the needs and desires generated by the father, impairs a simple identification of the mother with the good and restorative. In the oedipal dynamic, above all, the mother's position is inextricable from the father's, thus initiating the castration scenario. To go back even further and argue for a more primal 'wound', inflicted by absence of the breast, or Lacanian 'other', still demands some clarification of how this pre-oedipal imaginary space persists in the world of sexually differentiated adults. Luce Irigaray, for example, suggests that this exists in the 'thou' ('*tu*' in French) position, through which mothers and daughters can perform some repair to the damage caused by the intrusion of the oedipal phallic universe (1979, 1982, 1987).[23] Even she, though, does not pretend to render redundant the power relations associated with the oedipal processing of sexual difference: the 'thou' position certainly may subvert and further dislocate phallocentrism and offer new space for people to relate, but it will not remove overnight the power derived from set codes of sexual difference in a patriarchal socio-economic context (Irigaray, 1989).

Ferenczi was extremely conscious of these problems throughout his psychoanalytic career. Particularly important for him was how to incorporate some awareness of the 'patriarchal power' problem into psychoanalytic technique. First of all, how could the psychoanalyst learn to distinguish 'the love which the psychoneurotic patient *needs*', without appealing to an authority which is 'superior' to the love patients *think* they need (de Forest, 1954)? Even to restrict the superiority of the analyst's thought to the analytical situation – to justify it, for example, as the patient's projective identification of knowledge in the analyst – does not remove the epistemological issue of the status of the final curative 'experience' (*Erlebnis*), which supposedly removes neurotic symptoms (cf. Lacan, 1966, p. 28). Is this cure in some way polluted by that assumption of knowledge? Is the 'experience' just another 'insight' (*Einsicht*), another step in the same patriarchal knowledge system? Or is it different? Does the analyst's use of that assumption of knowledge actually expose and discredit the patriarchal power relationship on which it is based?

In answer to these questions, Ferenczi suggests that the experience analysts try to access is not only different from theoretical insight but fundamentally obstructed by it (cf. Haynal, 1988, p. 18). The central dilemma of psychoanalytic technique, therefore, is to form interpretations that will break down such obstruction, rather than reinforce it by endlessly theorizing around the patient's performances. Primarily, this means forging a new technique of interpretation, which will focus on and heighten the conflict between 'experience' and thoughts that cover it. Naturally, this applies equally to analyst and patient. Ferenczi's views on this technique developed throughout his career, but it is possible to observe a basic continuity from the initial 'free association' method to the 'active' analytical method, the 'relaxation technique' and 'mutual analysis'.

The 'free association' technique is a peculiar hybrid, because it derives from the different methods of treating hysteria formulated by Aschaffenburg, Freud, Breuer, Bleuler, Claparède, Cordes and Ziehen. Undeniably, though, its main development was pioneered by Jung in his 'diagnostic word association tests' from 1905–9. These tests were first seen as adjuncts to hypnosis; then, after 1906, as supplements to psychoanalysis. By 1909, their significance for psychoanalytic technique was paramount, as Jung's Clark University lectures well illustrate ('The association method' [1909] 1973, 2, pp. 439ff.). Basically, the test involved some four hundred 'stimulus-words', over half of which were nouns, a fifth verbs and a seventh adjectives (Jung and Riklin, 'The associations of normal subjects', [1905] 1973, 2, p. 5). Patients were asked to respond in whichever way they felt appropriate and the analyst timed and noted their response. It was assumed that the longer the patient took to react, the more profound was the unconscious material associated with the word. After the session, the analyst privately classified the types of association involved, ranging from 'repetition' of the stimulus-word to 'alliterative' and 'egocentric' reactions. From this, a nucleus of emotionally charged stimulus-words and responses could be traced out. Jung called these 'complexes' (1973, 2, pp. 526ff.). As the technique developed, patients were asked to explain why they had chosen their particular response-words. This, in turn, led to further associations.

The revolutionary factor in this was that it addressed the unconscious 'emotions' contained in patients' complexes and not the formal content of their verbal production. 'It has long been believed', Jung explained,

> that the association experiment enables one to distinguish certain *intellectual* types. This is by no means the case. The experiment does not give us any special insight into purely intellectual processes but rather into emotional ones. To be sure, we can establish certain types of reaction; they are not, however, based on intellectual peculiarities, but depend entirely on *emotional attitudes*. Educated subjects usually show trivial, well-canalized verbal associations, whereas the uneducated make more valuable, often more meaningful, associations. This behaviour would, from an intellectual point of view, be paradoxical. The associa-

tions, rich in content, offered by uneducated people are not really the products of a thinking rich in content but merely those of a particular emotional attitude.

(1973, 2, p. 458)

It is important to appreciate that Ferenczi's 'initiation' in psychoanalysis came through applying Jung's 'association tests'. He became fascinated by them in 1907, then apparently tried them out on all and sundry. Essentially, he always remained attached to the tests' basic aim of highlighting the 'emotional attitude' and subverting intellectual intervention. This carried over into his 'active', 'relaxation' and 'mutual' psychoanalytic techniques.

Like Freud, Ferenczi wanted to revise the artificial formality of the tests. Their principles could be preserved, especially the classification of associations, but the appropriate stimulus-words had to be discovered in the course of analytic sessions and re-introduced unobtrusively. This at least stressed the 'free' aspect of the associations. None the less, such 'freedom' was still vitiated by the analyst's 'superior knowledge'; the use of interpretation and classification was just more subtle, and the patient was simply manipulated – albeit in a supposedly benign, 'enlightened' way – to believe that such procedures were not taking place. The patients were then presented with the associative logic of their condition, as if it had emerged from the free play of words in analysis, rather than issuing from knowledge of a classification system. This renders the narrative of pre-1914 case histories particularly paradoxical: on the one hand, they stress the mistakes and open-endedness of the associative procedure and, on the other, they insinuate the peculiar inevitability of fixed symbolic correspondences (cf. Abraham and Torok, 1976; Bernheimer and Kahane, 1985; Mahony, 1984, 1987,

McCaffrey, 1989). This applies as much to Ferenczi's 'Little chanticleer' case (1913) as to Freud's 'Wolf man' (1914).

None the less, this particular form of 'free association' did not survive the First World War. The crucial transformative force was the large number of shell-shock victims psychoanalysts had to treat during the war (cf. Abraham *et al.*, 1921). Ferenczi assumed a distinguished role in this work, and became director of a special 'war neurosis' clinic in Budapest in 1916 (Ferenczi, '*Über Źwei Typen der Kriegsneurose*', *Zeitschrift*, 1917, iv, pp. 131–45). He argued that the main effect of shell-shock was to produce a psychotic splitting in which unconscious and infantile material erupted in the victims.[24] Analysis could comprehend this material, but its 'distanced and lengthy' technique was totally inappropriate. Above all, the victims needed active tenderness, so that they could relax enough for the analyst to communicate with their psychotic or split-off parts. In this context, time was desperately scarce, as there were hundreds of thousands of victims waiting for treatment, so frequent, intensive psychoanalytic sessions lasting months were out of the question. Even though the 'normal' duration of psychoanalysis then rarely exceeded a year, it was still necessary to shorten the treatment. Furthermore, the only medically recommended alternative at the time was electro-shock treatment, which was often used indiscriminately, permanently damaging many of the victims. In 1919, Freud attracted considerable hostility to psychoanalysis when he denounced this electro-shock treatment of war neuroses as an 'abuse' and a waste of electricity (Eissler, 1982).

At the first IPA Congress after the war, held in Budapest in September 1918, Ferenczi proposed the reform of psychoanalytic technique around the issue of the analyst's 'activity' in the analytical session ('On the technique of psychoanalysis', 1919, 2, pp. 177ff.). Analysts should be more 'active' in two specific directions. First, they should appreciate that some patients 'abuse' free association and use it to extend the psychoanalysis indefinitely, without ever breaking through to unconscious material. In these cases, Ferenczi argues, the analyst must break the 'fundamental rule', and direct the course of the analysis. To justify this, he employs an interesting analogy: 'The doctor's position in psychoanalytic treatment recalls in many ways that of the obstetrician, who also has to conduct himself as passively as possible, to content himself with the post of onlooker at a natural proceeding, but who must be at hand at the critical moment with the forceps in order to complete the act of parturition that is not progressing spontaneously' (1919, 2, pp. 182–3). The birth analogy ramified luxuriantly in this setting, particularly in Ferenczi and Rank's co-operation on technical 'development' – *Entwicklungsziele* implies an evolutionary *aim* in German (Ferenczi and Rank, 1986).

What Ferenczi meant by the 'active intervention' of the analyst was the imposition of certain tasks, to which the patient had to agree. If, for example, patients habitually failed to finish sentences, the analyst should ask them to agree to complete them as a matter of principle. If analysts felt that the patient was obfuscating through free association, then they should point this out and set a limit to the analysis in order to bring matters to a head. Of course, Freud had pioneered this method in the 'Wolf man case', not in the end with any great success (Freud, 1919a). Later, a similar principle was evoked in the Lacanian 'short session', again with controversial results.

Ferenczi also proposed forms of prohibition ('The further development of active therapy in psycho-analysis', 1920, 2, pp. 198ff.). This applied particularly to the obsessional masturbation substitutes employed by some patients during psychoanalytic sessions: clonic quivers of thighs, for example, rhythmic pressing of legs together, tongue-biting or chewing, nail-biting, beard-pulling or head-scratching. In some cases, though, Ferenczi would extend the prohibition outside the confines of analysis, and, for example, forbid the patient sexual intercourse (1920, 2, p. 214). He justified such prohibitions on the grounds that they would prevent the discharge of repressed libidinal energy, and hence heighten the tension in the session and bring unconscious material into sharper focus. The choice of prohibition, however, was not arbitrary. It should be informed by analysts' sense of areas in which unconscious material could not readily be accessed through free association, namely pre-verbal experience from early childhood. These areas were defined by the body-location of frustrated, damaged or denied – hence displaced – infantile drives. Careful location of prohibitions, therefore, should aim to provoke

> certain early infantile unconscious pathogenic psychic contents, which never were conscious (or preconscious) but which date from the period of 'uncoordinated gestures or magical behaviour', [which] cannot be simply remembered at all, but can only be reproduced by reliving in the sense of Freud's repetition. In this, active technique only plays the part of *agent provocateur*; its commands and prohibitions assist in obtaining of repetitions that must then be interpreted or reconstructed respectively into memory.
>
> (1920, 2, p. 217, original italics; the enclosed quote refers to Ferenczi, 1913, 1, p. 224)[25]

The second direction in which Ferenczi proposed to reform psychoanalytic technique was around due recognition of the phenomenon of countertransference ('The control of the countertransference', 2, pp. 186ff.). Freud had indicated this direction in 'The future prospects of psycho-analytic therapy' (1910d), when he made his celebrated declaration that 'no psycho-analyst goes further than his own complexes and internal resistances permit' (pp. 144–5). Initially, the problem of limiting the obstructions that such complexes and internal resistances imposed on psychoanalytic progress seemed easy to resolve; all analysts should first be analysed before they started practice. Ferenczi, however, felt that this also posed its own dangers.

> If the psycho-analyst has learned painfully to appreciate the counter-transference symptoms and achieved the control of everything in his actions and speech, and also in his feelings, that might give occasion for any complications, he is threatened with the danger of falling into the other extreme and of becoming too abrupt and repellent to the patient; this would retard the appearance of the transference, the pre-condition of every successful psycho-analysis, or make it altogether impossible.
>
> (2, p. 188)

The analyst, therefore, had to sense when to 'let go', and how to work with the countertransference to promote the dynamic unconscious relationship through which psychoanalysis advanced.[26] There were no hard and fast rules for this, just a warning not 'to overstep the right limits in either a positive or negative sense', that is, not to be too 'active' in expression of either love or hate for the patient (2, p. 189).

Again, in typical Ferenczi style, he was soon bothered by an apparent paradox between the two sides of his psychoanalytic reform programme: how could one suggest to analysts that they be active in the use of prohibitions as well as aware of 'becoming too abrupt and repellent'? His answer was to attempt to abandon all the coercive aspects of active technique. 'At length', he explained in 1925,

> I gave up altogether either ordering or forbidding my patients to do things, but now rather attempt to gain their intellectual understanding of the projected measure and only then put it into execution. In addition, I no longer bind myself so firmly in arranging these procedures that I cannot retract them sooner or later if the difficulties are insuperable on the side of the patient. Our 'active' mandates must therefore not be too rigid, but. . .be of an elastic compliancy.
>
> ('Contra-indications to the "active"
> psycho-analytical technique', 2, pp. 220–1)

Furthermore, he severely restricted his policy of setting a time limit to analysis.

> I was counting my chickens before they hatched, acting, that is, without a correct judgement of the possible stranglehold of the symptoms still existing – and so the fixed day for departure came without the patient being able to finish his treatment. There was nothing for me to do but to confess that my calculation was false, and it took me some time to dispel the bad impression of this incident under repeated hints of my ignorance. I learnt from this case not only that one must be extraordinarily cautious and only leave the beaten track on rare occasions, but also that one may only take on a mandate for this as for other 'activities' in agreement with the patient and with the possibility of retiring.
>
> (2, p. 222)

His revised 'active' technique therefore aimed to reduce as well as to increase tension: 'I have. . .learnt', he confessed, 'that it is sometimes useful to advise *relaxation exercises*, and that with this relaxation one can overcome the psychical inhibitions and resistances to association' (original italics, 2, p. 226). By 1929, relaxation had actually superseded tension as a means of gaining access to the unconscious.

> The extent to which patients improved when I employed this relaxation-therapy in addition to the older method was in many cases quite astonishing. In hysterics, obsessional neurotics, and even in neurotic characters the familiar attempts to reconstruct the past went forward as usual. But, after we had succeeded in a somewhat deeper manner than before in creating an atmosphere of confidence between physician and patient and in securing a fuller freedom of affect, hysterical physical symptoms would suddenly make their appearance, often for the first time in an analysis extending over years. These symptoms included paraesthesias and spasms, definitely localized, violent emotional movements, like miniature hysterical attacks, sudden alterations of the state of consciousness, slight vertigo and a clouding of consciousness often with subsequent amnesia for what had taken place.
>
> ('The principle of relaxation and neo-catharsis', 3, pp. 118–9)

Ferenczi believed that these symptoms released pre-verbal pleasures and pains that could issue only from 'definitely localized' body-sites. 'Under the method of relaxation', he explained, 'the hysterical physical symptoms have at times taken us back to phases of development in which, since the organ of thought was not yet completely developed, physical memories alone were registered' (3, p. 122).

Despite his obvious success with the relaxation technique, he still felt that it bore too strong a resemblance to hypnotic 'suggestion' (3, p. 134). No matter how 'flexible' and 'open' the analyst may be, the technique still essentially separated the analyst from the patient. The patient lapsed into this hysterical trance state and the analyst observed 'knowledge-ably'. There remained an element of denial of the counter-transference: the analyst resonated with the positive and negative aspects of the patient's transference, but followed the subsequent regressive trends only so far. At some point, the analyst switched off and resumed parental authority. 'Friendly encouragement', Ferenczi cryptically noted, '(possi-bly also some "electromagic") from another person, makes the removal of self-splitting possible and with it the "surren-der" as a reintegrated person. An "adult" is never "unsplit" – only a child and one who has again become a child. An adult must "take care of himself". A child is taken care of. *Trust* must be acquired analytically, by passing all sorts of tests set by the patient' (Note of 10 November 1932, 3, p. 270).

The paradox now shifted to the supposed power the ana-lyst derived from the patient's 'trust': if analysts had again 'become children' to remain in contact with their own and their patient's pre-verbal transference relationship, how could they suddenly emerge as the authoritative adult and still follow the trend of the unconscious 'experience'? Ferenczi's final answer was to reject the authoritative 'adult' position and advocate that the analyst accept the mutual regressive interac-tion of transference and countertransference.

> Certain phases of mutual analysis represent the complete renunci-ation of all compulsion and of all authority on both sides: they give the impression of two equally terrified children who compare their experiences, and because of their common fate understand each other completely and instinctively try to comfort each other. Awareness of this shared fate allows the partner to appear as completely harmless, therefore as someone whom one can trust with confidence.
>
> (*Diary*, 13 March 1932, p. 56)

In 'mutual analysis', the roles of analyst and patient could exchange, if both sides deemed it necessary. The analyst could also bring into the analysis whatever occurred within the countertransference. This could include negative as well as positive impressions. He would mention, for example, if a patient's smell offended him (*Diary*, pp. 123–4). He would also talk about his own sexual inadequacies (*Diary*, p. 164). Furthermore, the mutual exchange could accommodate pre-verbal tenderness, that is, touch and caress, where necessary. This was particularly appropriate with patients who had been brutally sexually abused as children, and needed to be held tenderly when regressed to that stage. Ferenczi totally rejected the charge that this could not but incorporate genital sexuality. For him, it was rather a precondition of mutual trust.

It would be totally ignorant to dismiss this technique peremptorily. First of all, it never set itself up as a definitive model, but rather as an experiment. It was the logical outcome of problems he encountered in the relationship between transference and countertransference in a clinical context, which he felt he could resolve only in this way. Ironically, and perhaps tragically, it led him far away from his original intention to shorten psychoanalysis and make it available to everyone. During mutual analysis, it was quite possible that an analyst would have time for only a single patient (Sterba, 1982). Finally, one should appreciate that the practice of this kind of 'love' did not go without extreme personal sacrifice. Not least, he had to face

> the possibility that people who are complete strangers to one will come into complete possession of my most intimate, most personal emotions, sins, etc. Consequently, I either have to learn to accept the impossibility, even madness, of this whole idea and technique, or I must go on with this daring enterprise and come

round to the idea that it really does not matter if a small group of people is formed whose members know everything about one another.

(*Diary*, 31 March 1932)

To follow the development of Ferenczi's theories of psycho-analytic technique does not afford much insight into his actual manner of practice. His psychoanalytic *style* remains concealed behind the closed doors of his consulting room. As with lovers – to follow his analogy – the particular *modus vivendi* involved cannot be reduced to a simple recipe or agenda. None the less, some stylistic flavour does issue from his diaries, letters and case notes which present accounts of analytic sessions. These are complemented by patients' ac-counts, which, although fragmentary, are extremely useful.

Most people with direct experience of Ferenczi's analytical skills speak of him as an unequalled virtuoso. Indeed, even the sternest of critics readily admits that his theories may perfectly well inform his own unique mode of practice; they are just not generalizable (cf. Sterba, 1982). Ernest Jones, for example, lists rather damning aspects of his own negative transference to Ferenczi; 'objective and critical judgment' was 'the one gift denied to Ferenczi'; he was 'unchivalrous in his attitudes to women'; and he also had 'rather masterful and even dictatorial tendencies' (Jones, 1959, p. 200). On the other hand, Jones tempered this with near adulation: Fe-renczi

> had an altogether delightful personality which retained a good deal of the simplicity and a still greater amount of the imagina-tion of the child; I have never known anyone better able to conjure up, in speech and in gesture, the point of view of a young child. These were invaluable qualities for psycho-analytic work, but he possessed others equally so. He had a very keen

and direct intuitive perception, one that went well with the highest possible measure of native honesty. He instantly saw into people, but with a very sympathetic and tolerant gaze. Then he had an exceptionally original and creative mind. His ideas were far too numerous for more than a small proportion of them to be committed to writing, so this quality could be fully appreciated only from repeated conversations with him.

(Jones, 1959, p. 200)

Ferenczi's special skill in psychoanalytic treatment was with 'hopeless and lost cases' (Balint, 1949). He took on the most difficult referrals and went to great lengths to give them his very best. He would see patients for hours and increase the frequency of sessions if necessary. Some of his analyses continued for a decade or more. For many years, he took his problem patients on holiday with him; only extreme fatigue and illness interrupted this in 1931 (cf. letter to Groddeck, 10 October 1931, Ferenczi and Groddeck, p. 123).[27] On the other hand, he had no rigid rules about the brevity of analysis either. He was quite willing to give single consultations or to take on severe cases for a few sessions. In this context, it is useful to observe the particular mix of positive and negative therapeutic results that such 'flexibility' provoked.

There is a fascinating account by Eleanor Burnet, of a brief analysis she had with Ferenczi in America in the winter of 1926–7 (1952, 1954). She suffered from a chronic phobia of daylight, combined with extreme anxiety fits, psychosomatic pains and fits of vertigo. 'From the beginning', she wrote, 'the rapport between Dr Ferenczi and myself as patient was excellent. The analysis proceeded, and material came through amazingly. But Dr Ferenczi was in this country for a limited stay, and he returned to Budapest while I was still far from being cured, for my neurosis was deeply rooted.' In other words, she clearly felt that the analysis did her good, but left her with a transference relationship that she could not replace.

> At long last I decided to give up trying to find the perfect successor to Dr Ferenczi and to live my life as well as I could, while ignoring my symptoms. It was, necessarily, a curtailed life, but not wholly an unrewarding one. Actually, although my fears were still like jack-in-the-boxes, I did build enough of a life to have a measure of satisfaction in it. But as for attempting to see beneath the surface without the aid of the transference I had with Dr Ferenczi, my recurrent *angst* was too terrible to attempt such a course.
>
> (1952, p. 162)

On reflection, it seems obvious that the analysis did not have the time to explore the negative aspects of transference. Moreover, even the awareness of the positive aspects tended to fuel her compulsion to flee. 'By now [after Ferenczi's departure]', she added,

> I was firmly convinced that analysis was my way out, and I was more than ever possessed of a dogged determination to recover at any cost to myself – or to any psychiatrist I could find. This period I call my time of 'escapes and hurried journeys'. Suffice it to say that I made some good tries, but with scant success. No one I found conducted an analysis on the same lines as had Dr Ferenczi, and since I had acquired the feel of the real thing, imitations merely discouraged me.
>
> (1952, p. 162)

Clearly, there is little point here in challenging the wisdom of a treatment that she considered improved her condition. None the less, serious questions must remain about what brief therapy can achieve without full analysis of the transference.

In contrast, the case of the 'Croatian musician' excellently illustrates the benefits of Ferenczi's willingness to improvise in the analytical setting (2, pp. 202–6). This is a case of a young woman who suffered from stage fright and a whole range of related phobias and obsessional states. She had difficulty, for example, walking in the street, or sitting among people, because she felt everyone was staring at her (imagined) too voluminous breasts. Consequently, she would fold her arms tightly across her chest to compress her breasts, but then became convinced that this just further drew attention to her condition. She was also convinced that she had really offensive breath and constantly consulted dentists and laryngologists, who always assured her that there was nothing wrong with her. Notwithstanding these difficulties, she could play the piano perfectly on her own and especially enjoyed performing prodigiously difficult finger exercises.

During one session, she mentioned a song which her elder, and somewhat tyrannical, sister liked to sing. Ferenczi encouraged her to sing the song there and then. After two hours, she managed to do this with great gusto and even imitated the expressive gestures of her sister. Thereafter, Ferenczi encouraged her to carry out any activities of which she was afraid, so she conducted orchestra pieces, imitating the sounds, or played the piano pieces she was afraid to perform in public. Ferenczi also encouraged her to write poetry and bring it to sessions.

Superficially, this would seem to contradict the fundamental principle of 'active' technique, namely to prevent the release of tension in sessions. In fact, the contrary is true: this illustrates rather the importance of distinguishing levels of disturbance and founding 'active' intervention on essential rather than peripheral problem areas. Ferenczi obviously sensed a deeper latent exhibitionist drive behind her performance anxiety, which centered notably on the exaggerated attention she gave to others' awareness of her imagined over-voluminous breasts. By encouraging her to perform, he brought this exhibitionist drive into sharp relief within the analysis: she came to see that 'she enjoyed displaying her various talents and that behind her modesty lay hidden a considerable desire to please' (2, p. 204). Her free associations subsequently shifted to her early conflict between onanistic fantasies and onanistic disgrace: this emerged around speculation on her performance of different, forbidden 'finger exercises' in private. Once this basic connection had been made, Ferenczi stopped the performances and literary production. At this point, she became intensely aware of the rhythmic play of her anal sphincter which she used to engage in during the performances. Ferenczi prohibited this play also, which subsequently provoked an intensification of her sense of bad breath. Inevitably, now, she made the connection between the punishment of anal play and its affective displacement to bad smells in her mouth.

The crucial technical question here is whether the encouragement to perform in sessions actually furthered the progress of the analysis in the way Ferenczi suggested. To orthodox analysts at the time, many of whom felt a handshake too demonstrative for an analytical setting, this degree of expressive freedom amounted to licentiousness (cf. Schmideberg, 1935). For Ferenczi, the transference and countertransference dynamic generated its own psychic space; only the analyst and patient could determine boundaries to expressive freedom or limits to temporal expansion. Clearly this woman needed to gain access to the roots of her stage fright, and attempting to perform in front of her analyst seemed a necessary preliminary to this. The site of the analysis, therefore, was justified by the particular aetiology of her symptoms.

In accounts of 'mutual analysis', Ferenczi's own presence and countertransference are much more evident. Decisions to be 'active' are made explicit and negative feelings clearly articulated. Perhaps the most documented 'mutual analysand' is Elizabeth Severn, to whom he refers alternately as 'my colleague' (at the Oxford Congress, 1929) and as 'Madame la Comtesse' (to Georg Groddeck).[28] Jeffrey Masson claims that she was a dancer at the time, but otherwise 'was not able to find out much about her' (1984, p. 161). In fact, as far as I know, she was American, had a doctorate in philosophy and was no stranger to psychoanalysis. In 1913, she wrote *Psychotherapy: Its Doctrine and Practice*, which ran to several editions (Severn, 1935). In this, she describes herself as a 'teacher and a healer', with 'considerable practical experience' in both (pp. 2–3). She followed this with *The Psychology of Behaviour* (1920), and *The Discovery of the Self* (1933), both of which rely heavily on her clinical experience.

She was in analysis with Ferenczi from 1924 to 1932. At first there were almost insuperable difficulties:

> When the case did not show any progress I redoubled my efforts; in fact I made up my mind not to be frightened off by any difficulty; gradually I gave in to more and more of the patient's wishes, doubled the number of sessions, going to her house instead of forcing her to come to me; I took her with me on vacation trips and provided sessions even on Sundays. With the help of such extreme exertions and the help, as it were, of the contrasting effects of relaxation, we arrived at the point where the evidently traumatic infantile history could emerge, in the form of states of trance, or attacks.
>
> (*Diary*, 5 May 1932, p. 97)[29]

This traumatic infantile history involved her having been drugged and sexually abused by her father at the age of eighteen months, then raped again at five years old. Following this abuse, according to Ferenczi, her 'orpha' – or organizing drive – focused around an assertive and rigorously routinized life-style: she displayed 'excessive independence and self-assurance. . .immensely strong will-power as reflected by the marble-like rigidity of her facial features. . .[and] altogether a somewhat sovereign, majestic superiority of a queen, or even the royal imperiousness of a king – all these are characteristics that one certainly cannot call feminine' (ibid., p. 97).

However, in mutual sessions, this assertiveness modified. 'In R. N. [Elizabeth Severn] I find my mother again', he wrote, 'namely the real one who was hard and energetic and of whom I am afraid. R. N. knows this, and treats me with particular gentleness; the analysis even enables her to transform her own hardness into friendly softness' (*Diary*, 24 February 1932, p. 45). She also helped Ferenczi in this way to gain certain insights into the countertransference:

> To my enormous surprise I had to concede that the patient was right in many respects. I have retained from my childhood a specific anxiety with regard to strong female figures of her kind. I found and continue to find 'sympathetic' those women who idolize me, who submit to my ideas and my peculiarities; women of her type, on the other hand, fill me with terror, and provoke in me the obstinacy and hatred of my childhood years.
> (*Diary*, 5 May 1932, p. 99)

Superficially, this obstinacy and hatred obstruct the analysis by exaggerating the importance of small details. His irritability, for example, is taken by her as a wish to kill or torture patients; her refusal or inability to pay fees is seen by him as a determined castration attempt (*Diary*, pp. 11, 193). On a deeper level, the countertransference completely disables him when he is faced with her anxiety attacks: 'In the case of

R. N. the attack would intensify until it reached an unbearable climax, and the patient would plead for help, often shrieking, "Take it away, take it away!" The appeal is obviously addressed to me, but it causes me the greatest embarrassment, since I have no idea of how I can help to relieve her state of suffering' (*Diary*, p. 106).

A fascinating and largely unexplored aspect of this case is their mutual interest in clairvoyance and thought transference. At first, Ferenczi distanced himself from her introduction of this issue into the analysis. 'With the help of an intermediary,' he reported, 'a Hungarian who at that time inhabited a distant land. . .the patient believes she discovered precisely me, through mystical thought-transference (n.b. 31 years ago), as the only person who would be able to help patients in great distress' (*Diary*, 24 February 1932, p. 43). Later he took it more seriously:

Patient R. N. even imagines at the time of the principal trauma, with the aid of an omnipotent intelligence (Orpha), she so to speak scoured the universe in search of help (by means of an ad hoc teleplastic organ). Thus her Orpha is supposed to have tracked me down, even at that time, as the only person in the world who owing to his special personal fate could and would make amends for the injury that had been done to her. This capacity of mine was unmasked in the course of mutual analysis as my sense of guilt at the death of a sister (diphtheria) two years younger than myself. The reaction against it makes me unsympathetic toward the sick; this I overcome by showing excessive kindness, medical interest, and tact (surely exaggerated). The analysis must establish the impatience behind this kindness and subtract it. Friendly feelings remain, that is, to some extent that Orphic fantasy is coming true.

(*Diary*, 12 June 1932, p. 121)

His changing view of the status of these 'ad hoc teleplastic organs' is particularly interesting: 'Expressed in psychiatric terms', he elucidated,

> *the hallucination* of breathing can maintain life, even when there is total somatic suffocation. The hallucination of muscles and muscular power, cardiac strength, evacuation of the bladder, vomiting, accompanying the complete paralysis of these organs, can delay the disintegration of the organism. The patients feel, however, that in a 'teleplastic' fashion, up to now perhaps believed in only by spiritualists, real organs, receptacles, gripping tools, tools of aggression are produced as ad hoc organs, which can take charge of a greater or lesser part of the organism's functions, while the organism is lying lifeless in a deep coma.
>
> (*Diary*, 9 June 1932, p. 117)

Elizabeth Severn's own particular ad hoc teleplastic organ was a bladder which formed at the back of her head to eliminate intense outbursts of pain.[30] 'The patient has the sensation that suddenly, at a painful spot at the back of her head, a bladder is formed, which has room for all her pain. The bladder is almost infinitely expandable. This is preceded by the actual elimination of a large quantity of urine. . . A more recent trauma can also overcome the bladder formation and cause it, so to speak, to burst' (*Diary*, p. 121). From this descriptive analysis, Ferenczi deduced the following clinical objectives: 'The seemingly impossible task here is (i) to refashion the bladder from its fragments (for which task the analyst is required to mobilize his intellectual powers as well as his patience to endure); (ii) to ensure that the bladder thus reconstructed reunites its contents with the ego (the body)' (*Diary*).

Clearly, Ferenczi came to regard this teleplastic organ as a crucial fantasy structure which could articulate split-off infantile fragments. As these were pre-verbal and pre-oedipal, they appropriated significant body sites. First of all, in the historical context, this structure may well have informed Melanie Klein's later notion of 'projective identification' (cf. her reference to Ferenczi in 'Notes on some schizoid mechanisms', [1946] 1975, p. 5). Second, such fantasy structures were 'clairvoyant' in so far as they processed the transference and countertransference in the psychoanalytic session. The 'cure' depended on utilizing the teleplastic organ to reveal its primal fantasy fragments, then to 'refashion' and 'reconstruct' itself in a unified body image. For the analyst, the organ negotiated the unconscious resonances with the patient and prompted the developmental form of the analysis; should it prompt 'embarrassment', Ferenczi requested the patient to assume the position of analyst.

Despite her powerful psychotic episodes, Elizabeth Severn's writing remained remarkably consistent. All her published work reveals a deep interest in spiritualist clairvoyance and the relationship between conscious and unconscious that is revealed in hypnosis. Of course, such a combination of interests was not unusual in the early years of this century. Edward Gurney and Frederick Myers had pioneered such an approach in the 1880s, and the Society for Psychical Research, which they helped found, published numerous cases of hypnotic revelation (Myers, 1935). Significantly enough, both Ferenczi and Freud were corresponding members of this Society.[31] It is not surprising then that Elizabeth Severn developed an early interest in psychoanalysis. 'Although I am not prepared to go the whole way in his views on the prevalence of sex perversions with Professor Freud', she wrote in 1913, '. . .I am constantly impressed with its importance as a primary cause in the larger number of cases of mental and nervous disorders' (p. 64). Interestingly enough, she modified, though never abandoned, this particular line. In 1933, after her analysis with Ferenczi, she contrasted the 'accepted psycho-analytic technique, which is purely dissecting in nature and which places its reliance chiefly on the mental grasp or "reconstruction" the patient can gain from his past', with 'a method which. . .does not scorn to "play mother" or be Good Samaritan to the injured one'. The latter method, which she relates to Ferenczi's 'relaxation principle', 'takes more time, it takes more patience, and it takes above all an emotional capacity or "gift" on the part of the analyst, who, unless he can do this, is not a true "physician of the soul"' (p. 95).

It is tempting here to interpret the later emphasis on trauma and the analyst's 'gift to play mother' as the direct effect of her analysis with Ferenczi (cf., Masson, 1984, pp. 165–6). Obviously, it would be foolish and inaccurate to deny that there was influence, especially after eight years of analysis, but it was a mutual influence, rather than a one-way process from Ferenczi to Severn. Severn certainly had intimations of 'active therapy' long before she encountered Ferenczi. In *Psychotherapy: Its Doctrine and Practice*, for example, she gave an extraordinary autobiographical example of her inability to face certain foods, which led to an eating disorder and an extremely abstemious diet (1913, pp. 52–3). She came to realize that she needed to find an appropriate form of action to come to terms with this disorder and prevent the syndrome from spreading. She decided to force herself to eat pancakes, the food she hated most. She was sick for the first two days but, on the third, managed to eat 'in peace and comfort'. 'From that day to this', she concluded, 'I have been free to eat what I choose at any time and of whatever nature, in perfect peace' (1913, p. 53).

Of course, with the hindsight gained from Ferenczi's *Diary*, the fantasy bladder can cast new light on her eating disorder; Ferenczi, for example, mentions her dream of 'a too big, but empty and withered breast' (19 January 1932, pp. 13–5). After associations, her disgust for this is related back to the forced fellatio she endured as a child. None the less, the manner in which she had earlier fixed on the digestive site of the repression, and evolved an appropriate prohibition and method of facing her problem, is strikingly similar to Ferenczi's 'active' technique. The unconscious fragments are not revealed by it, but the 'orpha' (organizing drive) is certainly facilitated in reinforcing the unity of the parts of ego that are left. To access these unconscious fragments, her 'orpha' would have to track down 'the only person in the world who owing to his special personal fate could and would make amends for the injury that had been done to her' (*Diary*, p. 121).

From his side, Ferenczi had to learn how to provide the 'love' that 'should be dispensed as an antidote to the pain (genuine compassion only, not feigned)' (*Diary*, 23 June 1932, p. 137). In Elizabeth Severn's case this was particularly difficult, given the strong negative countertransference. The only way to the right kind of love, then, was through analysis of this countertransference.[32]

> Profound self-analysis was required to uncover in myself the motives behind this antipathy, to paralyse it, and to strengthen my own character or, to put it better, my analytic potency, so that I would be able to help antipathetic people too. Aided by these measures, I became capable of engaging in battle with the demon that dominated the mind and body of the patient; while doing so, in a way demanding a great deal of intelligence and

ingenuity, I could drain away the patient's pain by my compassion. Through the continued application of such psychic drainage I could relieve the tension, which otherwise would tend to explode, to a point where encouragement to reach insight and conviction became increasingly possible. Nevertheless success and progress, though quite evident, were dreadfully slow.

(*Diary*, 23 June 1932, p. 137)

Ironically, Severn's fantasy bladder intrudes metaphorically even in this narrative: the 'love' here defined contains a peculiar amphimixis of the sexual ('analytic potency'), the spiritual ('the demon') and the urinary ('psychic drainage').

Chapter 6

Teratoma

I can picture cases of neurosis – in fact I have often met with them – in which (possibly as a result of unusually profound traumas in infancy) the greater part of the personality becomes, as it were, a teratoma, *the task of adaptation to reality being shouldered by the fragment of personality which has been spared. Such persons have actually remained almost entirely at the child level, and for them the usual methods of therapy are not enough.* What such neurotics need is really to be adopted and to partake for the first time in their lives of the advantages of a normal nursery.

—Sándor Ferenczi, 1929, 2, p. 124, original emphasis

WE ARE STILL not sure how the mind lives in the body or the body lives in the mind. We are not even sure whether the notions of 'mind' and 'body' adequately account for our experience. We may want to introduce more subtlety: like Jung and Hillman, for example, to situate both 'mind' and 'body' in a range of terms like 'soul', 'imagination' and 'syzygy' (Jung, 1959, 9[2]; Hillman, 1972, 1975, 1985); or, like Winnicott, to replace the body/mind split by 'psyche-soma', so that the psyche may become integral to 'the imaginative elaboration of somatic parts, feelings and functions, that is, of physical aliveness' ([1949] 1987, p. 244).

In the clinical context too, contemporary diagnostic categories strike precarious balances between 'psychological' and 'physical' determinants. Particularly problematic here is the category of disorder entitled 'psychological disorders affecting physical condition' (DSM-III[R], 1987, p. 333). Here 'demonstrable organic pathology (e.g. rheumatoid arthritis) or a known pathophysiologic process (e.g. migraine headache)' are partially provoked or exacerbated by 'psychologically meaningful environmental stimuli' – by which is meant phenomena like the death of a relative, loss of a lover, or redundancy. A patient, though, may well display the same symptoms – including vomiting, abdominal pain, nausea, diarrhoea, heart palpitations and chest pain – but have no such apparent 'meaningful' environmental cause. In this case, all 'standard laboratory procedures' should first be tried. If these produce no results, then one is entitled to 'conceptualize by psychological constructs only' (ibid.).

Even in the case of 'purely psychological disorders', distinctions operate on the physical level. 'Conversion disorders' (which are sometimes referred to as 'hysterical neurosis – conversion type') involve paralysis of limbs, aphonia or blindness (ibid., p. 257). The 'psychological' causes here are usually vague: the disorder is 'apparently an expression of psychological conflict or need' (ibid.). Most cases of this rare disorder, however, do relate to a specific, though perhaps not 'psychologically meaningful', environmental stimulus, namely the effect of warfare (ibid., p. 250).

In contrast, 'somatization disorder' involves 'recurrent and multiple somatic complaints, of several years' duration, for which medical attention has been sought, but that apparently are not due to any physical disorder' (ibid., p. 261). These differ from 'conversion disorders' in so far as they involve varieties of pain, as opposed to paralysis or loss of function of limbs, ears, eyes and vocal cords. Again, the 'psychological' causes here also manifest themselves physically, usually through sexual disorders like impotence, pain during intercourse, or sexual indifference.

Obviously, psychoanalytic treatment of both conversion and somatization disorders conveniently tends to assume that there is no primary 'organic' reason for the given symptoms and that the 'psychological' enquiry can at least promise diagnostic clarification, if not cure. None the less, the decision to remove the 'organic' to secondary diagnostic status usually remains tentative. Analysts sometimes worry that they have missed a crucial organic factor underlying the patient's condition: Freud illustrates this fear perfectly in the dream of Irma's injection (Freud, 1900, 2, p. 374).[33] Furthermore, the assumption of purely 'psychological' causes takes for granted some direct transmission into physical effects, such as pain or paralysis. The actual form of that transmission – or how it articulates psychological material in specific body locations with particular intensity – is usually ignored.

One method of clarifying the issues at play here is to examine the diagnostic discourse about it. This involves studying its nosological development in the context of allied analytical procedures, such as those applied to neurological, endocrinal or behavioural systems. Such a study need not be integral to psychoanalytic practice – that is, form part of psychoanalytic training – but it is necessary critically to relate psychoanalytic discourse generally to the numerous discourses that construct the clinical situation. It should be stressed that these discourses are neither necessarily homogeneous nor necessarily predominantly scientific. The metaphor of illness, for example, subverts any desired exclusion of the clinical from the everyday setting. Social discourses predispose patients to view illnesses as judgements or punishments, particularly where death may intrude – as in the case of cancer, syphilis or AIDS (Sontag, 1977, 1989). Treatment therefore cannot avoid popular fears and interpretative processes, particularly in so far as they affect reaction to treatment patterns.

Unfortunately, the subtleties of discourse analysis were not available to the early analysts. They generally still tended to believe in a simple 'organic' foundation for mental illness, even if they could not readily identify it. Alfred Adler, for example, proposed 'myelodysplasia', or 'organ inferiority', as a prime cause for neurotic and psychotic disturbance (Adler, 1909). According to this, individuals were born with specific organ weaknesses, which predisposed them to certain illnesses, unless they compensated 'psychologically', that is, became aware of their inferiority and constructed appropriate life-styles. Similarly, Otto Gross proposed 'organic degeneration' as the basis for all mental illness and outlined a dual prototype of the 'pathologically inferior' and the 'genius' (Gross, 1909). The genius could compensate for such organic inferiority through creative work, but the less gifted had to adopt cruder forms of protest, such as violence and crime.[34]

In contrast, Ferenczi became increasingly distanced from simple 'organic causal' explanations of mental illness. He could not accept, for example, that the 'small penis complex' related simply to organic 'fact', as opposed to persistent infantile perspectives; nor could he dismiss sexual 'perversions' as organically, as opposed to oedipally, fashioned. Never the less, he persisted in his belief that 'psychoanalysis, like every psychology, in its attempts to dig to the depths, must strike somewhere on the rock of the organic' (2, p. 377). By this, he wished to draw attention to the peculiar use that psychoanalysis made of organic terminology to explain psychological conditions – particularly 'trauma', which denotes an organic as well as a psychological wound, but also the extensive incorporation of contemporary neurological terminology (such as the 'cathexis' [*Besetzung*] metaphor accom-

modating 'drive', 'object' and 'innervation'). Such terms func-
tioned as analogies, so contained both organic and psychological referents. A trauma, for example, might refer to a
specific psychological event such as a rejection or insult from
someone, but it might also be articulated physically in a pain,
numbness or dizziness. These different levels of reference
within analogies did not necessarily bargain or 'reckon'
(*Rechnen*) with each other to create an easy coexistence or
predominance of one connotation over another. On the contrary, their illustrative power often derived from their con-
flictual meaning in given contexts: use of organic metaphors
could serve to highlight basic doubts about organic functioning in general. Ferenczi argued, for example, that Freud's
definition of consciousness as a 'sense organ for unconscious
psychic qualities' simply highlighted the ambiguities involved
in interpreting the metaphorical function of the term 'sense
organ': did it indicate passive reception of unconscious qualities or did it convey their filtering and inhibition? Could even
'sense organs' perform both functions? Ferenczi concluded
that Freud chose the term 'sense organ' precisely to open up
such multiple interpretations, as well as possible grounds for
approaching tensions in 'consciousness' itself (Ferenczi, 'The
psyche as inhibiting organ', 1922, 2, pp. 379–83).

Perhaps the most challenging use of biological analogy
was formulated by Ferenczi's close friend, Georg Groddeck.
Groddeck proposed to link the organic with the unconscious
in the form of the 'Id' or 'It' (*Das Es*). This provided an
appropriate subject position within language – the third person singular – and therefore encouraged purposeful linguistic
and literary links with organic processes. This was particularly the case with illness, which Groddeck interpreted analogously as a psychosomatic expression of the 'Id'. 'Sickness',
he wrote, 'is. . .a symbol, a representation of something

going on within, a drama staged by the It, by means of which it announces what it could not say with the tongue. . .every sickness, whether it be called organic or "nervous", and death too, are just as purposeful as playing the piano, striking the match, or crossing one's legs. They are a declaration from the It' (Groddeck, [1923] 1935, p. 117).

Ferenczi was fascinated by this view, but sceptical about the direct causal link between psychic condition and illness. Particularly worrying was the strictly determined direction from the 'id' to the 'ego', which gave neither room nor power to change through consciousness. Typically, Ferenczi chose to illustrate this feature of Groddeck's work by focusing on his use of language. Groddeck, he felt, overused the term 'therefore'. In the Groddeckian system, the 'Id' speaks, therefore the ego experiences: 'man does not live, but becomes "lived" by a "therefore"' (Ferenczi, review of Groddeck's *Der Seelensucher*, 1921, *Bausteine*, 4, p. 154).

In contrast, therefore, Ferenczi proposed two kinds of 'psychic' conversion of symptoms into 'illness': the 'autoplastic' and the 'alloplastic' conversion (*das Auto- und Alloplastik*). The autoplastic conversion was the first ontogenetic and phylogenetic form of psychic reflex, which did not affect later psycho-physiological developments that linked the ego instrumentally with the outside world. Autoplastic forms of psychosomatic illness therefore formed around basic internal vital processes: the hysterical lump in the throat, painful constipation and mock pregnancies were prototypes of this (Ferenczi, 'The phenomena of hysterical materialization', 1919, 2, pp. 89ff.). The 'alloplastic' form of conversion developed within the 'fort-da' negotiation of the external world, so framed itself within the ego's terms of using reflex responses to negotiate its wishes and desires: the prototypes here were loss or impaired use of limbs, sexual impotence and hysterical blindness, muteness and deafness (ibid.).

Despite such basic theoretical revisions, Ferenczi remained delighted by Groddeck's use of various narrative forms to display the fictional potential of 'illness'. Groddeck's *Der Seelensucher* (The Soul Searcher), for example, was a novel; *Das Buch vom Es* (The Book of the It) was an 'imaginary psychoanalytic correspondence' from a doctor to a friend. Particularly striking for Ferenczi was the evocation of how early infantile destructive drives colour popular representations of fatal illness: 'the word "cancer",' wrote Groddeck, 'like the word syphilis, is spoken and printed a hundred times a day, for what do men love to hear better than ghost stories? And since one can no longer believe in ghosts, these two names, still indefinable in spite or by reason of so much scientific knowledge, which call up so much that is grotesque and horrible in their associations, provide a good substitute for grizzly spectres' ([1923] 1935, p. 118). Groddeck, in fact, derived great significance from the fact that the word 'cancer' denotes both the illness and the crab ('*Krebs*' in German conveys this more emphatically than English, where the crab figures only in cancer as the astrological sign). He links the fact that the crab walks backwards to repressed 'primal scene' dread that parents copulate like animals, that is, *a tergo*, or backwards. The fact that the crab has shears similarly links to 'the great anxiety problem of castration'; this both reactivates the pain of the cut of the umbilical cord, and the horror of menstruation, which symbolically bleeds the blood of the severed penis (Groddeck, [1923] 1935, p. 119).

Although Ferenczi rejected the determinism of this – namely Groddeck's view that 'what is not fatal is not cancer' ([1923] 1935) – he did value the metaphorical space it generated. He particularly appreciated the invocation of the primal fantasy scenes, notably the identification of denial of parental copulation and castration as a primary impulse towards somatization.[35] Ferenczi's main doubts here, however, were that the products of this denial should *necessarily* somatize or become malignant. For this reason, he preferred to use the term 'teratoma' (*Teratom*) to that of cancer. Medically, a teratoma is a tumour, made up of various types of tissue, which may or may not be malignant. In a literary context, the term recalled Groddeck's evocation of 'horror stories': teratomae here were a special kind of monster, either constructed from parts of different bodies, like Frankenstein, or emerging from a person's fantasy and physically transforming them, as in the case of Dr Jekyll and Mr Hyde. Such monsters suited Ferenczi's purpose, because they embodied projections of isolated fragments and destructive fantasy drives. Naturally, they could remain primarily imaginary – as in the cases of false pregnancies or hysterical lumps in the throat. The choice of the term 'teratoma', therefore, articulated the denial of parental copulation and castration in two distinct ways: autoplastically, it formed tumours, and, alloplastically, it raised monsters and doubles.[36]

Perhaps the most important implication of this choice of term was that it stressed dependency on primary life-drives, which meant that it could be removed without necessarily jeopardizing life in general. 'It is no more poetic licence', Ferenczi wrote, 'to compare the mind of the neurotic to a double malformation, something like the so-called *teratoma* which harbours in a hidden part of its body fragments of a twin-being which has never developed. No reasonable person would refuse to surrender such a teratoma to the surgeon's knife' (1929, 3, p. 123). Unlike Groddeck's formulation,

therefore, it was possible for the analyst to operate psychically and foster the life process: there was no intractable
death-drive which excluded psychological intervention in its
organic progression.

An important and perhaps *terminal* context, in which to
locate Ferenczi's use of 'teratoma', is that of his own experience. By his own admission, he was extremely prone to
psychosomatic illness: he suffered periodically from tachy-
cardia, insomnia, nocturnal apnoea, and asthma (which he
called his 'angsthma'). Curiously, he associated these with
the 'will to die' and chose none other than Groddeck to
consult for treatment in August 1921 (cf. letter to Groddeck,
discussing his complaints, 19 February 1923, Ferenczi and
Groddeck, pp. 84–7). Indeed, in 1923, he developed a 'teratoma', a goitre, which he discussed with Groddeck at the
same time as he wished to 'deliver' into the world the Thalas-
sal theory of genitality (letter to Groddeck, 9 June 1923,
ibid., p. 88). With Groddeck's help, Ferenczi interpreted the
various symptoms as isomorphic with infantile destructive
drives: these intruded 'psychically' into his sexual life – dis-
rupting 'coital satisfaction' – and somatized into various
anxiety 'ingrowths' (ibid., p. 86). A strange horror story,
corollary to this diganostic debate, was Ferenczi and Groddeck's discussion of Freud's cancer, which was first diagnosed at precisely this time (Ferenczi to Groddeck, ibid.,
p. 87). Groddeck offered several times to treat Freud but was
always politely refused. In contrast to Ferenczi's case, there
were no speculations on the infantile psycho-sexual origins
of somatization, only a description of surgical intervention
and a long inventory of pain (Ferenczi to Groddeck, 25
October 1923, p. 93).

* * *

To conclude, I propose to explore a further possible ramification of the 'teratoma' analogy. Let us assume that inner growths and outer doubles are not all bad. The prototypes here could be the foetus and the ideal-ego.[37] Now one could argue that there is considerable narrative confusion surrounding the growth of these prototypes. In miscarriage, for example, women's bodies sometimes 'read' pregnancy as an illness, hence develop antibodies against the foetus (cf. Ferenczi, 2, p. 93). Similarly, psychoanalysts 'read' ideal-egos as 'dangerous' unconscious identification with heroic types, that can promote psychotic negation of the real world (Laplanche and Pontalis, 1980, pp. 201–2). None the less, the final products are assumed generally to promote life rather than death – namely, the infant from the foetus and the super-ego from the ideal-ego.

To proceed a step further: let us assume that the psyche is 'pregnant' with ideas and that the progress of this pregnancy is determined by identification with ideal-egos. Analogously, therefore, the growth of the 'teratoma' will be threatened by antibodies and psychotic negation. Critical questions will emerge and the contributions of the identified 'heroic types' will be split or denied. How then to operate? Obviously, one way would be to facilitate the birth of the conscious creative individual while cutting away negative teratomic effects. Analysis of the growth of the teratoma therefore serves to separate out 'good' and 'bad' aspects, ending with an elastic set of principles, and an agency, the super-ego, through which to negotiate productive relations between the inner and outer world (cf. Ferenczi, 'The elasticity of psychoanalytic technique', 1928, 3, pp. 87–101). In contemporary terms, therefore, the teratoma analogy can be viewed as a 'transitional object' which negotiates a relationship between the growth of ideal-ego ideas in oneself and the outside 'influence' of inner systems of thought (cf. Winnicott, 1971). In this context, then, it is possible to trace the teratomic mix of good and bad in inner and outer growths of Ferenczi's ideas in the lives and work of those he influenced.

In a controversial paper delivered to the American Psychoanalytic Association in New York on 28 December 1926, Ferenczi attempted to assess his own teratomic effect (cf. 3, pp. 29–40). In this he proposed 'a kind of menu, which as you know is not a thing to satisfy hunger. My aim is merely to arouse in you a desire, the satisfaction of which can only come through the study of the original works' (p. 29). In other words, to proceed further, one had to 'eat' – that is, introject! For starters, the menu listed 'active technique', then proposed suitable gastronomic routes through the main course.

Two routes were highly recommended: the criminal treatment programme and the child analytic process. The first traced an appropriate growth of active method in the treatment and care of criminals. In this context, Ferenczi's pupil, Franz Alexander, argued that the relaxation method was particularly successful in uncovering the infantile sources of violent and criminal drives (Alexander, 1933, pp. 189ff.).[38] A similar approach was proposed by August Aichorn in 1921 for the treatment of borstal boys at St Andrä in Austria (Aichorn, 1925). Aichorn believed that traditional punishment methods only confirmed people in their criminal behaviour and closed them to any meaningful psychoanalytic exchange. Punishment was what they expected, but, if this was refused and unconditional love offered instead, they would be caught off their guard, thus opened to psychoanalysis. Only such 'active' expression of love could promote the necessary, psychoanalytically informed, curative environment (Aichorn, 1976).

Alexander's teratomic development of Ferenczi matured into the concept of the 'corrective emotional experience'. He described and justified this as follows:

> The parental intimidation is corrected by the more tolerant and sympathetic attitude of the therapist, who replaces the authoritarian parents in the patient's mind. As the patient realizes that his modest self-assertion will not be punished, he will experiment more boldly. At the same time, he can express himself more freely toward persons in authority in his present life. This increases the ego's capacity to deal with aggressive attitudes which anxiety had previously repressed.
>
> (Alexander, 1960, pp. 286–7)

On the positive teratomic side, the concept of 'corrective emotional experience' clearly incorporated the main ingredient of Ferenczi's recipe, namely that the patient should be offered the love and tenderness of which they had been deprived (cf. de Forest, 1954). Alternatively, on the negative teratomic side, the concept missed the 'elasticity' of Ferenczi's active method. Ferenczi was well aware that patients could stall the analytical progress precisely because they fed on the analyst's love rather than working on their own experience. In short, 'corrective emotional experience' could easily degenerate into a new kind of dependency (Ferenczi, 1925, 2, p. 221). Hence the need, at times, to temper such psychoanalytical love with agreed self-imposed limitations and prohibitions on the patient (Ferenczi, 1925, 2, pp. 217–29).[39]

Ferenczi's influence in the second recommended 'gastronomic route', child psychoanalysis, is less acknowledged, therefore potentially more controversial. Phyllis Grosskurth suggests, for example, that he considered child analysis 'a suitable endeavour for a woman', implying that it was either unsuitable or demeaning for men (1986, p. 74). It is certainly

true that he did not regard child analysis as his own special-
ity, but he none the less felt it was perfectly concordant with
active technique. 'My former pupil, Mrs Klein of Berlin', he
wrote, 'has taken the first courageous step in this field. She
analysed young children and infants with the same fearless-
ness as we do the adult. She observed the children during
their play, and used my method of forced fantasy or imagination much in the same sense as I advised with adults, and
found that neurotic and problem children can be helped by
symbolic interpretations and explanations' (3, p. 38). Furthermore, it is obvious from his seminal work on child development that he both undertook extensive infant observation
and did treat child and adolescent patients (cf. 1, p. 213; 2,
p. 391; 3, pp. 30–55). For him, most important was the *range*
of experience that bore upon the subject, including, notably,
adults' relationships to their childhood, socially sanctioned
child-rearing practices and kindergarten rituals and regula-
tions (Ferenczi, 'The adaption of the family to the child – free
associations on children's education', 1928, 3, pp. 61–70).

How then to assess Ferenczi's teratomic influence on his
'ex-pupil', Melanie Klein? It can be established from her
unpublished notes that she was an assiduous and conscien-
tious pupil, as she read his work extensively and carefully.[40]
She also sent all her early papers to him for comment. She
asked for advice, for example, on how to present case material on her son, Eric, as well as requesting books and further
advice on reading (cf. unpublished letter from Klein to Ferenczi, 14 December 1920, Melanie Klein Trust, London). It
is clear too that her play technique and views of super-ego
formation were formulated in direct response to Ferenczi's
work. What remains to be established, then, is the negative
teratomic dimension – or where to locate the clear rejection
of Ferenczi's views in her psychoanalytic position.

Significantly, the focus for the growth of their differences formed precisely around the conception of how the psyche accommodated infantile destructive drives. For Ferenczi, like Freud, the problem of 'adaptation' (*Anpassung*) to destruction was encapsulated in the term 'restitution' (*Wiederherstellung*), which denoted literally putting the pieces back together again after the destructive event. Klein also uses the term 'restitution', but rarely. She contrasts it with her preferred term, 'reparation' (*Wiedergutmachung*), by which she denotes paying life-long dues for destructive drives; the pieces are not put together and the situation is not restored to its original state.

First of all, it should be mentioned here that this distinction between 'restitution' (*Wiederherstellung*) and 'reparation' (*Wiedergutmachung*) is not generally recognized by Klein scholars. Grosskurth, for example, suggests that 'reparation' becomes important only in 'late' Klein; in fact, she even claims that Joan Riviere was the first to elaborate on the subject in 1936 (Grosskurth, 1986, pp. 235–6; Riviere, 1937). Grosskurth also repeats Dr Boulanger's claim that Klein 'could not care less for the preservation of the historical development of her ideas' and cites in evidence her permission to allow the French '*réparation*' to translate 'restitution' in the French edition of her work (Grosskurth, 1986, pp. 391–2). In fact, the French translators – one of whom, significantly, was Jacques Lacan – did not follow Alix Strachey's mistranslation, but correctly reflected the German original. Indeed, it becomes obvious from comparing Strachey's translation with Klein's original *Die Psychoanalyse des Kindes* (1932) that the centrality of 'reparation' is totally absent in the English: '*Wiedergutmachung*' is rendered by 'restitution' and '*Wiedergutmachungstendenzen*' by 'restitutive tendencies' (compare, for example, p. 169 in the English text with p. 178 in the German, and pp. 247–8 in the English with pp. 257–8 in the German). This error has misled prominent English-speaking Kleinians, notably Donald Meltzer, to argue that Klein used the term 'restitution' exclusively until 1946, when, he claims, she apparently launched a 'new' concept of 'reparation' (Meltzer, 1978[2], p. 44).[41]

The German term '*Wiedergutmachung*' (reparation) has a special connotation that is not readily discernible in English. It was used to describe the life-long payments, or 'War Reparations', that Germans had to make first to the Allies after the First World War, then to Holocaust survivors after the Second World War. This connotation clearly weighs heavily on the term's conceptual use in the psychoanalytic context. It reinforces Klein's intention to denote major, interminable dues, that neither remove guilt nor promise any short-term gain or improvement (cf. Klein, 'On the theory of anxiety and guilt', [1948] 1975, 4, p. 41).

It is this connotation that marks the teratomic difference between Klein and Ferenczi. Clearly, both accept the full implications of the death-drive for psychoanalytic theory and practice. Ferenczi, in fact, claims to have introduced the notion to Freud in the first place (Ferenczi, 'To Sigmund Freud on his 70th birthday', 1926, 3, p. 16). Ferenczi also discusses 'regenerative tendencies' (*Wiederherstellungstendenzen*) which need to be fostered by active technique in the analytic context (3, pp. 230–1). In *this* sense, Kleinian 'reparation' could be said 'actively' to foster the 'depressive position' (or desirable recognition of the mix of positive and negative in everything – though not, of course, in manic or obsessional reparation). The difference, though, is that Kleinian reparation is life-long and, by definition, cannot secure a permanent option on the 'depressive position': no one can permanently balance out 'good' and 'bad' objects and avoid paranoid-schizoid splitting, although persecutory and depressive anxiety can be reduced through reparative 'mourning' (cf. Klein, 'On the criteria for the termination of a psycho-analysis' [1950] 1974, 4, pp. 43–7).

In contrast, Ferenczi argues that analysis does facilitate 'the discovery and eventual control of certain otherwise inaccessible nuclei of repression' (Ferenczi, 'The problem of the termination of the analysis', 1927, 3, p. 85). Evidently, this does not 'cure' all ills, but places the patient in a position where the 'regenerative tendencies' outweigh the destructive ones. This position is reached when the patients themselves are 'regenerated' enough to see that they no longer need analysis. In certain circumstances, 'active' participation could even precipitate the patient's reaching this point – for example, by setting a time limit to the analysis. The rationale here is that the exhaustive analysis of every trauma in its peculiar amphimixic presentation is unnecessary if reasonable control of the 'nuclei of repression' is consolidated. This allows Ferenczi to pioneer short-term analysis, whereas Kleinian analysis normally lasts years.

It is irresistibly tempting to situate this particular difference in the context of Klein's analysis with Ferenczi. Ironically, this continued for some six years, albeit intermittently (1912–9). There is little available documentation of this, though Klein did comment briefly on it in her unpublished *Autobiography*. It is notable here that she makes a point of stressing that Ferenczi encouraged positive transference, but totally ignored negative transference. 'Technique at this time was extremely different from what it is at present [1953] and the analysis of negative transference did not enter. I had a very strong positive transference and I feel that one should not understate the effect of that, though, as we know, it can never do the whole job' (Klein Trust manuscript, p. 42).

Curiously, this bears a striking resemblance to Ferenczi's comments on his own analysis with Freud. 'I particularly regretted', Ferenczi wrote to Freud, 'that you did not notice in me and bring to abreaction the negative feelings and fantasies. Painstaking self-analysis was therefore required which I subsequently undertook and carried out quite methodically' (unpublished letter of 17 January 1930). To terminate appropriately with an open speculation: did perhaps both Ferenczi's and Klein's views of how to approach destructive drives develop teratomically around the same significant absence in their personal analyses?

* * *

It is possible to pose, but not answer, some questions, because there is too little information or no available sources; or perhaps because the question needs to be lived with, and allowed to suggest different, perhaps contradictory directions. A person's work can be neither closed to further interpretation nor rid of its contradictions – many of which may be interesting in their own way. It disseminates itself variously in other people's spaces, in other languages and cultures. You read everyone's work in the same way as you read the patient on the couch. You do not try to categorize and enclose them from the start with set theories and interpretations. You try as best you can to appreciate what gives them space; you follow their language and movements to trace out auto- and allo-plastic shapes. After all, then, digging and cutting is a co-operative process. It is neither pre-indicated nor set to a superior design. It shifts and approximates to support whomever it can. The reader, writer, analyst and patient need support. They move on up the line to those who offer love. Along the road, for sure, they will encounter a few malignancies and a few monsters. If they have a friend or lover, at least they will discover their own way to intervene. If not, the tumours will erupt and the monsters wreak havoc. Or, at least, that is the way Ferenczi started his analytical narrative.

Peroration

I HOPE THAT this book has illustrated Ferenczi's extra-ordinary scientific range and vivid creative imagina-tion. It should also have substantiated grounds for a re-appraisal of his importance. We have seen that he pioneered psychoanalytic research in early infant develop-ment and helped formulate the first forms of child analysis; he introduced the notion of the analyst's 'active' intervention to promote the progress of treatment, which later inspired 'focal' or 'brief' psychotherapies; he promoted the incorpora-tion of psychoanalysis in educational programmes, both by arguing for a broad cultural training for analysts and by inaugurating psychoanalytic studies programmes in higher education; and, finally, he campaigned for a psychoanalytic form of sexual enlightenment, which would replace fear and punishment of purportedly 'degenerate' or 'deviant' sexuality by care and understanding. In short, therefore, he must now be valued as a crucial innovative figure in the development of psychoanalysis, whose insights can continue to inspire future psychoanalytic work.

One major question remains to be answered: why has so little of this been previously appreciated? We have seen that Ferenczi did not flinch before unpleasant, even devastating truths and constantly revised his work accordingly. This is particularly the case with child sex abuse, whose importance he reconsidered throughout his life. He did not simply *note* the fact that many more people were sexually abused than previously thought, but set about understanding this occurrence in a way that could further the care and treatment of all concerned. Thus, he effectively countered those whose response is simply to punish the abuser or to insist on the intractable sexual 'innocence' of the child. He insisted, rather, on distinctions between 'rape' and 'seduction', and on the importance of the difficult area that contemporary mental health professionals designate as 'inappropriate fondling'.

Obviously, such truths are not easy to accept. Analysts, like the general public, often prefer clear-cut, seemingly uncontroversial categories and approaches. They also favour thinkers who appear secure with their categories and set in their ways. It is surely alarming for some to read an analyst who is disturbed and challenged by the reality that emerges in the consulting-room. Similarly, it is unsettling for some to co-operate with a person who constantly wishes to improve their ways of working with that reality. Ferenczi, then, like all such self-declared 'restless spirits', has been greeted so far with the classic response of feigned indifference. Fortunately, though, it is not easy to will away the relevance of such insight. I hope, therefore, that this book will help foster a fresh appreciation of the substance of Ferenczi's work.

Notes

1. By 'anarchic', I do not refer to terrorism, or violent protest, but to a philosophy which promotes 'mutual aid', 'co-operation', and the appreciation of 'difference', rather than power and authority (cf. Kropotkin, *Mutual Aid: A Factor of Evolution*, 1902).

2. It is important here to note the influence of Hans Vahinger's *The Philosophy of 'As If': A System of the Theoretical, Practical, and Religious Fictions of Mankind* (1897) on the early psychoanalysts. This is acknowledged and discussed by Alfred Adler in *Über den Nervösen Charakter* [1912] 1972, pp. 54ff.).

3. Herbert Silberer (1882–1923) is an interesting but almost totally forgotten early psychoanalyst. His work on dream processes inspired all those working in the area, especially Freud, Jung, Ferenczi and Stekel (cf. M. Stanton, 1988, p. 164).

4. One should mention here Janet's pioneering work on the importance of mirrors and mirroring in *Névroses et idées fixes* (1898, 2, pp. 486ff.), which in turn inspired (among others) Ferenczi, Freud, Jung and Lacan.

5. This recalls Winnicott's meditations on transitional phenomena and transitional objects (Winnicott, 1971).

6. For confusion in the English translation of 'instincts' and 'drives', see Laplanche and Pontalis, 1980, pp. 214ff.

7. Charcot's pupil, Joseph Babinski, carried out extensive tests on this parallel, and considered epilepsy, sleep and orgasm as similar spinal reflexes.

8. Ferenczi stressed the importance of movement profiles in diagnosis (cf. 'Thinking and muscle innervation', 2, pp. 230ff.).

9. The linguistic form of this displacement is metonymy, in which a part displaces the whole; for example, the term 'sail' can displace 'boat' – 'there are thirty sails in the fleet' – or the term 'bottle' can displace wine – 'let us drink a few bottles' (cf. Jacques

Lacan, 'The agency of the letter in the unconscious or reason since Freud', 1977, pp. 156ff.).

10. It is interesting that Phyllis Grosskurth implies that Ferenczi supported Anna Freud against Melanie Klein in the last years of his life, and, indeed, that 'The confusion of tongues' paper 'was contrary to all she believed' (Grosskurth, 1986, p. 200n). In support of this, she cites the Circular Letter (*Rundbrief*) of 30 November 1930. In fact, in this, the Budapest 'group' is invoked, not specifically Ferenczi. Within that group, Klein had one fierce and influential opponent, Sándor Rado. Furthermore, Ferenczi had previously addressed the differences between Anna Freud and Melanie Klein on several occasions, notably at a meeting in London in 1927 (Ferenczi, 3, p. 69). Here he consistently referred to Klein as his 'pupil', who 'courageously applied his principles'. He categorized Anna Freud's views as 'more conservative', though he hoped that both views could be 'brought together' (3, p. 69; cf. 3, pp. 127ff.). As far as Klein's and Ferenczi's theoretical positions were concerned, I hope this book illustrates that there are more parallels than was previously thought.

11. For Bion, the alpha function converts primary sensory material into meaningful thought contents. When it fails, the sensory material remains as 'beta elements', which are processed by projective identification (Bion, 1967, pp. 110–19).

12. Cf. the 'age' and 'types of abuse' categories and correlations used by the Great Ormond Street Sexual Abuse Team (Bentovim et al., 1989, pp. 19, 21, 31).

13. Cf. Ron Williams's pioneer work in this area (unpublished papers and MA dissertation, University of Kent, 1989).

14. According to Bentovim et al., 'inappropriate fondling' is numerically the most prevalent and the most problematic 'type of abuse' (op. cit., p. 19).

15. In Masson's *own* translation of this passage, he realigns the text to suggest that the first sentence involving 'seduction' stands on its own, so that all the rest appears to be qualified by it (Masson, 1984, p. 289).

16. Ferenczi wrote this in 1926, long after most people had forgotten about the importance of Sabina Spielrein's seminal arti-

cle '*Die Destruktion als Ursache des Werdens*' (1912). Spielrein's view of the formative role of infantile destructive drives in structuring the ego prefigures Klein's elaboration of the 'depressive position' (cf. Klein, 1975, pp. 253–4).

17. The alternative view is cogently expressed by Luce Irigaray, who regards the elaboration of sexual differences as an enrichment, rather than the doomed violation of 'natural' frontiers (Irigaray, 1989).

18. The work of Martha Davis casts new and interesting light on non-verbal cues in psychotherapy (cf. K. and M. Stanton, 1989).

19. Critics have been disturbed particularly by suggestions that Anna Freud may have had a lesbian relationship with Dorothy Burlingham; that Karen Horney may have been promiscuous for long periods of her adult life and even slept with students; and that Melanie Klein may well have seriously affected (her daughter) Melitta Schmideberg's sex life, to the point of driving her to marry an allegedly impotent, homosexual, alcoholic drug addict.

20. The distinction between '*Einfall*' and '*Assoziation*' is not immediately apparent in the English edition of Laplanche and Pontalis (1980, p. 41, and pp. 169–70). It is however usefully clarified by Laplanche through the notion of 'idée incidente':'. . .*Einfall* is distinguished from *Assoziation* by the disconnected nature of the context. . .' (Bourguignon *et al.*, 1989, p. 108).

21. Poul Bjerre (1876–1964) is an important but ignored figure in the early psychoanalytic movement. Like Ferenczi, he discovered Freud through Jung's word-association tests and a general interest in hypnotism as a therapeutic model. He followed Jung in leaving the IPA, and developed an independent psychotherapeutic tradition in Sweden. There is an interesting published exchange of letters between him and Jung over Jung's Presidency and general role in the 'international' section of the German Medical Psychotherapy Association during the Nazi era (cf. Jung, 1973).

22. Ferenczi defined the relative value of 'active technique' against both Adler's and Jung's positions (cf. Ferenczi, 1925, 2, pp. 213ff.; cf. Adler, 1929).

23. Irigaray's expositions of the 'thou' tend to be poetic (cf. *Passions Élémentaires*, 1982).

24. Shell-shock was previously studied as 'battle hysteria'. In 1918, Babinski and Froment even suggested the phenomenon be incorporated within the general notion of 'suggestion'. They also believed that it was contagious (cf. Merskey, 1979, p. 37).

25. The choice of the term *'agent provocateur'* is interesting here, given that this refers to a spy who enters an enemy or criminal community to force the guilty to reveal themselves. This exposes the paradox of the 'good' that has to use force to express itself.

26. Developments along these lines have pursued the theme of countertransference as projective identification (see Robert M. Young, unpublished paper, University of Kent, March 1990).

27. It should be noted that taking patients on holiday was not an unusual practice at this time!

28. One should also mention the other 'mutual analysand' who figures prominently in the *Clinical Diary*: 'Dm.'. She is, in fact, Clara Thompson, who later helps found the Association for the Advancement of Psychoanalysis in New York and works closely with Erich Fromm, Karen Horney and Harry Stack Sullivan.

29. Throughout the *Clinical Diary*, Elizabeth Severn is referred to as 'R.N.'.

30. This is one of the frequent sites of teratomae.

31. Apparently, Ferenczi actually contributed a paper to the Society which was not published because it was considered to be too obscene.

32. Self-analysis is central to Ferenczi's psychoanalytic technique (cf. the autobiographical 'Dream of an occlusive pessary', 1915, 2, p. 204).

33. Some critics assume that Freud's 'malpractice' began with his use of cocaine (cf. Masson, 1984; Thornton, 1983).

34. There is an interesting exchange of views between Freud and Jung on Gross's opinion: Freud says it is 'paranoid' (3 June 1909) and Jung claims it expresses Gross's fight against his father (4 June 1909) (Freud and Jung, 1974, pp. 227–9).

35. Sontag (1977) indicates how tuberculosis was supposed to have a sexual aetiology.

36. The classic teratomic 'double' is Oscar Wilde's Dorian Gray (cf. Rank, 1971, pp. 71–4).

37. The Jungian analogy is the animus/anima (cf. Hillman, 1985).

38. In 1932, Franz Alexander founded the Chicago School and introduced these methods in training.

39. Comparisons are possible here with Winnicott's notion of the 'facilitating environment' (cf. 'The anti-social tendency', [1950] 1987, pp. 306–15); cf. 'the notion of re-mothering', Krzowski and Land [eds.], 1988).

40. The Melanie Klein Trust, at the Wellcome Library, London, hold some of Klein's reading and case notes. These continue in German until well after her initial formulation of the 'depressive position' (1935). There are also drawings and notes of patients' movements.

41. In contrast, Bob Hinshelwood does relate the concept to the early period, but does not mention the German distinction with '*Wiederherstellung*' (1989, pp. 396–400).

Glossary

INCLUDED HERE ARE only the terms which are especially associated with Ferenczi and which remain unexplained, or inadequately explained, elsewhere. For Freudian and general psychoanalytic terminology, the reader is referred to Laplanche and Pontalis's *The Language of Psychoanalysis* (1980) and Laplanche's *Terminologie raisonnée* (1989). Following this tradition, I have placed the original German after the terms used in the English edition, and note any apparent disparity. For the problems inherited from the Strachey edition of Freud, I refer the reader to Darius Ornston's seminal paper, 'Strachey's influence: a preliminary report' (1982) and subsequent discussions (Timms and Segal, 1988; Special Issue, *International Review of Psycho-Analysis*, pt. 2, 1990).

ACTIVE TECHNIQUE
(*Aktiventechnik*)

The psychoanalytic method Ferenczi introduced in 1919 to prevent the 'abuse of free association'. This initially consisted of setting a time limit to the psychoanalytic treatment and imposing certain agreed prohibitions on the patient, notably regarding sexual activity. The aim here was to 'heighten the tension' in the analytic session, and thus to precipitate the disclosure of unconscious material. In 1920, the method broadened its scope to include encouraging the patient to give voice, draw or dramatically represent material that caused anxiety.

THE "AHA" EXPERIENCE
(*Aha-Erlebnis*)

This is the moment when intellectual understanding (*Einsicht*) combines with emotional experience (*Erlebnis*), and the full meaning of an important factor in life emerges. In the psychoanalytical setting, it is when a number of interpretations connect and 'dawn' on patient or analyst in a major way. They feel tremendous physical pain, joy or release, as well as major insight into their lives.

THE ALLOPLASTIC AND THE AUTOPLASTIC
(*Allo- und Auto-plastik*)

The dual form of psychosomatic adaption (*Anpassung*). The auto-plastic is the early infantile, pre-oedipal form, which expresses 'body memories', that is, experiences which are not verbally mediated. As such, it follows, modifies and disrupts internal bodily processes. The hysterical 'lump in the throat' (*globus hystericus*), 'false pregnancies,' and tumours are prototypes here. The allo-plastic form is a later, post-oedipal development. It therefore shapes itself symptomatically around interactions with the external world. The prototype here is failure, paralysis or part-disablement of those organs that negotiate 'outer space' (sic.) for us, namely eyes, ears, vocal cords, hands, arms or legs (cf. Laplanche and Pontalis, 1980, pp. 48–9).

AMPHIMIXIS
(*Die Amphimixis*)

A medical term denoting the mingling of two different substances to create a third, whose main example is the fusion of
sperm and ovum to create the foetus. Ferenczi uses this
analogously to describe the combination of different eroticisms, relating to different psycho-sexual development
stages, that make up every sexual 'act'. In this sense, there is
no irreversible progression of sexual experience to 'normal'
coitus, rather a 'mix' of infantile, adult, oral, anal and genital
components. The balance of the 'mix' alters according to the
specific confrontation between inner and outer world encountered in infancy and latency: rape or seduction during
childhood, for example, lead to major imbalances, usually
denying all else to preserve pre-oedipal psycho-sexual modes
of gratification. Similarly, the 'mix' has no prescribed auto-,
homo- or hetero- object choice; it tends, according to circum-
stance, to incorporate variously all three. The choice of analogy therefore draws attention to a basic flaw in the notion of
natural unilinear sexual development. The infinite number of
acts of coitus, and the consequent preservation of the species,
cannot contain 'regression', that is, the appeal of earlier oral
and anal modes of gratification. Amphimixis, then, negotiates an uneasy unity.

AUTOSYMBOLISM
(*Autosymbolismus*)

This is a term that Ferenczi borrowed from Herbert Silberer
to denote symbolism that reflects psychic processes them-

selves. There are three autosymbolic prototypes: the machine, the mirror and the bridge. These symbols negotiate tensions between the inner and outer world. Such negotiations are not simple, as they stem the primal defences of introjection and projection. Hence they are constantly subverted by 'inner' and 'outer' vicissitudes; machines, for example, project our inner organic processes to the point where they assume some 'outside' dimension that we can control – we cannot readily switch off our bowels, for example, but we can switch off the washing-machine; likewise, mirrors reflect so much of the 'outside' world that they become paradigms of our 'inner' production of the 'outside' – Janet, Wallon and Lacan, for example, appeal numinously to this symbol to constitute primary consciousness; last, but not least, the bridge, whose ability to 'transfer' is taken for granted, but whose original construction plan and pre-ordained traffic flow seem irresolvably controversial – take language (or 'word bridges'), for example: few are intrepid enough to decide conclusively whether anyone starts out with the primary irreducible 'inner' language and crosses over into 'outer', everyday, intersubjective language or whether it is the other way around (Steiner, 1978; Lacan, 1966).

HATE
(Hassreaktion, Wutregungen gegen der Analytiker)

Ferenczi uses the term 'hate' ambivalently. On the one hand, 'hate' articulates the death-drive and sets in motion primordial destructive and restitutive forces. It provokes, for example, the whole process of 'displacement' (*Verschiebung*). Alternatively, 'hate' is purely reactive and sometimes contains justifiable anger. This is particularly the case in analysis, where the patient can feel rage (*Wut*) at the analyst's insensitivity.

LANGUAGE OF TENDERNESS AND PASSION
(*Die Sprache der Zärtlichkeit und der Leidenschaft*)

Tenderness is the pre-oedipal and passion the post-oedipal register of experience. Tenderness therefore tends to focus on oral gratification, kissing, nuzzling and snuggling close together. Passion is phallic, incestuous, hence prone to punishment (castration) and laden with guilt ('*Leiden*' means 'to suffer' in German).

Ferenczi concentrates on the 'confusion' (*Sprachverwirrung*) of these two registers in the relationships between adults and children: in many 'seduction' scenes, children desire tenderness and adults respond passionately.

LOVE
(*Liebe, Verliebtheit, Lieben*)

A big noun (*Liebe*), which Ferenczi uses in two distinct ways. First, as a positive transference phenomenon, in which the subject is entranced by the object of desire. This focuses on reception of a dominating experience, as the hypnotized experiences the hypnotizer. In German, this use is always qualified by the passive – '*Verliebtheit*' refers to the state of 'being' in love, rather than actively 'loving'.

In contrast, the verb to love 'actively' (*Lieben*) defines the analyst's task, which defies coercion and instead offers the patient tenderness (*Zärtlichkeit*). This active form is difficult to define, precisely because it is neither dominating nor based on patriarchal authority within the oedipal model. Instead, it is inspired by the mother's position, which is purposefully defined as separate from the then socially accepted views of women as passive receptors of phallic penetration (Ferenczi, *Diary*, 26 November 1932). Ferenczi is quite aware that this begs many political questions, and indeed implies that everyone should explore such questions through study of contradictions in the mother's position.

MUTUAL ANALYSIS
(*Mutualismus*)

The final development of 'active' technique (1929–32), which involves exchanging places between analyst and patient where this seems fruitful. Ferenczi stresses that this principle cannot be generalized. It depends entirely on carefully nurtured trust and mutual regression to the language of 'tenderness'.

ORPHA
(*Orpha*)

This term derives from spiritualist terminology, where it denotes creative destiny (following Orpheus, the god of poetry and imagination). This concept emerges late in Ferenczi's career, largely in response to his mutual analysis with Elizabeth Severn. For him, it indicates the unconscious, vital, organizing instincts that nourish people and prevent them from falling apart during moments of severe crisis.

PLAY
(*Spielen, Lutscheln*)

For Ferenczi, like Freud, 'play' is the primordial form of learning which attempts to control the absence of gratification through pictorial, verbal and body language (the fort–da game). It is therefore a drive (*Spieltrieb*) which patently fails in its aim to design the external world to fit the requirements of the inner world. Instead, it further displaces the desired gratification through its own symbolic networks. Hence, the free-associative game (*Handlungsfreiheit*) which playfully tries to catch itself out and reflect back on the original game-plan that generated so many displacements.

RECKONING
(*Rechnen*)

The psychic process of negotiating between unconscious determinations and conscious will-directed intentions in the world. The term carries connotations of haggling over bills and precarious distinctions between subjective impression and objective 'fact'. As such, one constantly has to 'reckon' with both inner and outer worlds; one has to argue one off against the other to establish known ground on which to assess the effect of action.

RELAXATION TECHNIQUE
(*Relaxionsprinzip*)

The second phase of 'active technique', introduced in 1925, which suggests nurturing and calming exercises in analysis to contrast with the prohibitions of the earlier phase. Relaxation technique is particularly recommended with patients who have suffered early infantile trauma.

UTRAQUISM
(*Utraquismus, Utraquistische Arbeitsweise*)

The Utraquists were a sixteenth-century Protestant sect who derived their name from the Latin '*utraque*', meaning 'one and the other' or 'both'. This applied to their belief that the laity should have the right to take both bread and wine in the communion, thus destroying the privilege of the clergy and reuniting the blood and flesh of Christ in the people. It is curious, then, that this term should have such resonance for Ferenczi, an agnostic Jew. Perhaps there was an identification with Jan Hus, who was born not far from Ferenczi; he similarly suffered from reactionary imperialists, and was burned at the stake in 1415. More likely, there was a reference to Jung's views on 'communion' as the primal analogy for the symbolic 'kiss' between priest's penis and female penitent's vagina in early pagan ceremonies (Jung, 1919, p. 86).

Anyway, Ferenczi uses this term to describe his theory of analogy. According to this, it is possible to draw productive parallels between seemingly distant areas of research, such as poetry and physics or drama and biology. The 'meaning' derived from such analogies is 'associative', that is, dependent on the value derived from the interpreter(s) and not on the set legitimation of either discipline.

VENTRILOQUISM
(*Bauchreden*)

This denotes the unconscious 'voicing' of anxieties by patient's bodies. Twitching, nervous coughs, obsessive leg-crossing, ear- or nose-boring, nail-biting, farting, sweating or a frequent need to go to the toilet illustrate this phenomenon.

THE WISE-BABY PHENOMENON
(in English in original, and *gelehrter Säugling*)

This relates to a common dream in which babies speak with great wisdom about the world. Ferenczi views this as illustrative of the 'clear-sightedness of the uncorrupted child'. The 'wise baby' voices the 'language of tenderness' which often lies repressed beneath numerous layers of the 'language of passion'.

Bibliography

FERENCZI, SÁNDOR

OR THE TEXTUAL references here to the original German edition and English translation, see introductory notes, p. xi. It should be noted that there is an important discrepancy between the two editions. Ferenczi's mother tongue was Hungarian, though much of his work was written in German. There are therefore articles in Hungarian which remain untranslated into any other language. (In this context, readers are referred to the Hungarian Ferenczi Society, which can be contacted through Dr György Hidas, The President, Sándor Ferenczi Society, Szilaasy út 6, H-1121 Budapest, Hungary.) There are also German articles which remain untranslated into Hungarian or English. The main bibliographic references here are in Volume 2, pp. 451–69, and Volume 3, pp. 377–86, of the English edition; in the German edition, the main bibliography is in Volume 4, pp. 298–327.

Ferenczi co-authored with Otto Rank *The Development of Psycho-Analysis*, published in New York and Washington in 1923 by the Nervous and Mental Disease Publishing Co. Ferenczi's review of Rank's *Technique of Psycho-Analysis* is in *The International Journal of Psycho-Analysis*, 8, 1927, pp. 93ff.

The following are the main texts unreferenced and untranslated in the English edition:

1899

Hypospadiasis ritkább esete (A rare case of hypospadiasis)
Pemphigus esete (A case of pemphigus)
Strictura recti esete (A case of strictura recti)
Furunculus gyógyítása (The treatment of boils)

1900

Hyperdactylia esete (A case of hyperdactylism)

1901

A szerelem a tudományban (Love in the sciences)

1902

Megligyelesek agyverzesek es gyoyitasuk korul (Observations on strokes and their treatment)
Homosexualitas feminina (Female homosexuality)

1903

Encepalopathia saturnina (Homosexual brain pathology)
Cretinismus két esete (Two cases of cretinism)
Izomhüdésekkel szöv dölt tabes (Muscular paralysis in a case of locomotive ataxia)
Facialis bénulás infectiosus alapon (Facial paralysis with infectious causes)
Szoptatástól kiváltott thyreogen tetania (Tetanus provoked through silence)

1904

Adat a Trousseau-tünet újabb magyarálatához (A report on new information on trousseau-symptoms)

A tápkészitmények diaetetikus értékéröl (On the dietary value of patent foods)
Tetania-esetek (Tetanus cases)
Ataxia hereditaria (Hereditary ataxia)
A hipnózis gyógyito értekéröl (On the therapeutic value of hypnotism)

1905

Agyalapi törés ideghüdéssel és arcgörccsel (Cranial fracture with nervous paralysis and brain seizure)
Hozzászólás Schaffer Károly: 'Az agyi érzészavarokról klinikai és anatomiai szempontból' c. elöadásához (Discussion of Karl Schaffer's lecture on 'Cerebral parathesias in the clinical and anatomical contexts')
Egy anya és hároméves gyermekének tetania-tünetei (Tetanus symptoms in a mother and her three-year-old child)
Részegség megállapítása hullából (Confirmation of intoxication in a corpse)
Nothnagel (Obituary)

1906

Polyneuritis ritkább esete (A rare case of polyneuritis)
Jegyzetek Dr Dumas (Ledignan) 'Levelek az orvosi pályára készülö ifjúhoz' eimen a Gyógyászatban megjelent eikkekhez (Memorandum on Dr Dumas's 'Letter to a young person who wants to become a doctor')
Conjugált szembénulást utánzó szemizomhüdések (Eye paralysis leading to eye muscle paralysis)
Az idegorvoslás recepturá jához (On the reception of nervous healing)

1908

Polyneuritikus sorvadás (felkar és alszár izmainak) (Bicep and calf muscle atrophy)

Baleseti sérülés okozhat-e progressiv paralysist (Can accidental injuries bring about progressive paralysis?)

1909

A balesetbiztosítási intézmény kilátásairól és a balesetinidegbántal makról (On the views of insurance companies concerning nervous illness after accidents)

Az álom psychoanalysise és annak kórtani jelentösége (On the psychoanalysis of dreams and their pathological meaning)

Rf. Kenyeres Balázs dr 'Törv'nyszéki Orvostan' (On Dr B. Kenyeres's *Forensic Medicine*)

1910

Lélekelemzés, Értekezések a pszichoanalizis köréböl (Psychoanalysis: essays on the areas covered by psychoanalysis)

Review: Dr M. Farkas, '*Über die Kombination von Hydro- und Psycho-therapie*' (On the combination of hydro- and psychotherapy)

Dr E. Jendrassik, '*Über den Begriff der Neurasthenie*' (On the notion of neurasthenia)

Dr Fülop Stein, '*Tatbestandsdiagnostische Versuche bei Untersuchungsgefangenen*' (Attempts at evidential diagnosis with prisoners on trial)

Dr Eduard Hitschmann, '*Freud's Neurosenlehre*' (Freud's theory of the neuroses)

1911

Anatole France als Analytiker (Anatole France as psychoanalyst)

Alcohol und Neurosen (Alcohol and neurosis)

Review: Dr O. Dornblüth, *Die Psychoneurosen* (The psychoneuroses)

1912

A tudattalan megismerése (Understanding the unconscious)
Lelki problémák a pszichoanalizis megvilágitában (Psychic problems in the light of psychoanalysis)
Preface to Hungarian version of Freud '*Über Psychoanalyse*' (On psychoanalysis)
Review: Dr J. Brenner, '*Az elmebetegségek psychikus mechanismusa*' (The psychic mechanisms of mental illness)
Prof. L. M. Bossi, '*Die gynäkologische Prophylaxe bei Wahnsinn*' (Gynaecological prophylaxis in madness)

1913

A psychoanalysisröl és annak jogi és társadalmi jelentöségéröl (On psychoanalysis and its legal and sociological importance)
Aus der 'Psychologie' von Hermann Lotze (From Lotze's 'Psychology')
Az idegkörtanban értékesithetö néhany megfigyelés a szemen (Valuable neurological information from the eye)
Reviews: A. A. Brill (general review of 'Freud's theory of compulsion neurosis'; 'Psychological mechanisms of paranoia'; 'Hysterical dreamy states, their psychological mechanism'; 'A few remarks on the technique of psychoanalysis'; 'The only or favourite child in adult life'; 'Analeroticism and character' (*Zeitschrift*, 1913, 1, pp. 180ff.)
Morton Prince, 'The meaning of ideas as determined by unconscious settings', (*Zeitschrift*, 1, pp. 185ff.)
C. G. Jung – *Kritik der Jungschen 'Wandlungen und Symbole der Libido'* (A criticism of Jung's 'Symbols of Transformation of the Libido') (*Zeitschrift*, 1, pp. 391–403)

1914

Büntények lélekelemzése (The psychoanalysis of burglary)
Ideges tünetek keletkezése és eltünése és egyéb értekezések a pszi-

choanalzis köréböl (Origins and disappearance of neurotic symptoms in psychoanalysis)

Review: E. Bleuler, '*Kritik der Freudschen Theorie*' (Critique of Freudian theory)

C. G. Jung, '*Contribution à l'étude des types psychologiques*' (Contribution to the study of psychological types)

M. Steiner, '*Die psychischen Störungen der männlichen Potenz*' (The psychic disturbances of male potency)

H. Flournoy, '*Épilepsie émotionelle*' (Emotional epilepsy)

R. Weber, '*Rêverie et images*' (Dreaming and images)

P. Bjerre, '*Das Wesen der Hypnose*' (The essence of hypnosis)

G. Berguer, '*Note sur le langage du rêve*' (Note on dream language)

E. Partos, '*Analyse d'une erreur scientifique*' (Analysis of a scientific error)

F. Meggendorfer, '*Über Syphilis in der Aszendenz von Dementia Praecox Kranken*' (On syphilis in the growing importance of 'dementia praecox' illnesses)

1915

Die Psychiatrische Schule von Bordeaux über die Psychoanalyse (The Bordeaux psychiatric school on psychoanalysis) (*Bausteine*, 4, pp. 12–45)

A veszedelmek jégkorszaka (The ice-age of dangers)

Preface for Freud *On Dreams*

A 40–50 évesek sorozása (The acceptance of 40–50-year-olds)

Agysérüléses katonák utókezelése (On the after-care of brain-damaged soldiers)

Reviews: J. Kollarits, '*Observations de Psychologie Quotidienne*' (Observations of daily psychology) and '*Contribution à l'étude des rêves*' (Contribution to the study of dreams)

P. Schilder and H. Weidner, '*Zur Kenntnis symbolähnlicher Bildungen im Rahmen der Schizophrenie*' (On the knowledge of symbolically representative pictures in the framework of schizophrenia)

L. Buchner (pseud.), '*Klinischer Beitrag zur Lehre vom Ver-*

hältnisblödsinn' (A clinical contribution to the theory of ratio-
nonsense)
C. G. Jung, '*Psychologische Abhandlungen*' (Psychological essays)
E. Claparède, '*De la représentation des personnes et des lapsus
linguae*' (On the representation of people and slips of the
tongue)

1917

'*Ostwald über die Psychoanalyse*' (Ostwald on Psychoanalysis)
(*Zeitschrift*, 1916–17, 4, pp. 169ff.)
Barátságom Schächter Miksával (*Meine Freundschaft mit Max
Schächter*) (My friendship with Max Schächter)
Review: Dr I. Décsi, '*Ember, mért vagy ideges?*' (People, why are
you so nervous?)
A. Adler and C. Furtmüller, '*Heilen und Bilden*' (To heal and
educate)
E. Bleuler, '*Physisch und Psychisch in der Pathologie*' (Physical
and psychological in pathology)
L. Kaplan, '*Psychoanalytische Probleme*' (Psychoanalytic prob-
lems)
J. J. Putnam, 'The work of Adler'
J. H. Schultz, '*Freuds Sexualpsychoanalyse*' (Freud's sexual psy-
choanalysis)
E. Claparède, '*Rêve satisfaisant un désir organique*' (Dream satis-
fying an organic desire)

1918

'*A mese lélektanáról*' (On the psychology of fairy tales)

1919

Hysterie und Pathoneurosen (Hysteria and pathological neurosis)
'*A pszichoanalizis haladása*' (The development of psychoanalysis)

1920

Review: J. Schaxel, '*Abhandlungen zur theoretischen Biologie*' (Essays on theoretical biology)

A. Lipschütz, '*Die Pubertätsdrüse und ihre Wirkungen*' (Pubertal glands and their operation)

E. Landau, '*Naturwissenschaft und Lebensauffassung*' (Natural science and the interpretation of life)

H. Strasser, '*Fragen der Entwicklungsmechanik*' (Questions of the mechanics of development)

Otto Gross, '*Drei Aufsätze über den inneren Konflikt*' (Three essays on inner conflict)

1922

Review: Karl Abraham, '*Klinische Beiträge zur Psychoanalyse*' (Clinical essays on psychoanalysis)

Raymond de Saussure, '*La méthode psychanalytique*' (Psychoanalytic method)

1923

A psychoanalysis a gyakorló orvos szolgálatában (Psychoanalysis for general practitioners)

Verzeichnis der wissenschaftlichen Arbeiten (Index of scientific work)

Ferenczi-Festschrift der *Internationalen Zeitschrift für Psychoanalyse* (volume dedicated to Ferenczi), 1923, vol. 9, part 3

Preface to Hungarian edition of Freud's *Psychopathology of Everyday Life*

1924

Altató és ébresztö tudomány (Sleep-inducing and invigorating science)

Ignotus, a megértö (Hugo Ignotus, the understanding. . .)

1925

Charcot (in *Bausteine*, vol. 4)

1929

Psychoanalysis és constitutio (Psychoanalysis and constitution)
Vorbericht und Schlussbemerkungen zu 'Aus der Kindheit eines
Proletariermädchens, Aufzeichnungen einer 19 jährigen Selbst-
möderin über ihre ersten zehn Lebensjahre' (Introduction and
final observations on 'From the childhood of a working-class girl:
notes of a 19-year-old suicide case on her first ten years of life')

1930

A 'psychoanalysis' név illetéktelen használata (On the unjustifiable
use of the label 'psychoanalysis')
'Viszonválasz' Dr Feldmann válaszára (Reply to Dr Feldmann's
reply)

* * *

Reviews of the following books/articles are contained in Volume 4
of the *Bausteine*, but remain untranslated in English:
E. Jones, *Papers on Psycho-Analysis* (1913)
A. Maeder, *Sur le mouvement psychanalytique* (1913)
A. A. Brill, *Anal-eroticism and Character* (1913)
───── *The Only or Favourite Child in Adult Life* (1913)
E. Bleuler, *Kritik der Freudschen Theorien* (1914)
C. G. Jung, *Contributions à l'étude des types psychologiques* (1914)
M. Steiner, *Die psychischen Störungen der männlichen Potenz* (1914)
R. Weber, *Rêverie et images* (1914)
P. Bjerre, *Das Wesen der Hypnose* (1914)
G. Berguer, *Note sur le langage du rêve* (1914)
F. Meggendorfer, *Über Syphilis in der Aszendenz von Dementia*
Praecox Kranken (1914)
J. Kollarits, *Observations de psychologie quotidienne* (1915)

—— *Contribution à l'étude des rêves* (1915)

P. Schilder and H. Weidner, *Zur Kenntnis symbolähnlicher Bildungen im Rahmen der Schizophrenie* (1915)

L. Buchner, *Klinische Beitrag zur Lehre vom Verhältnisblödsinn* (1915)

E. Claparède, *De la représentation des personnes inconnues et des lapsus linguae* (1915)

C. G. Jung (ed.), *Psychologische Abhandlungen*, vol. 1 (1915)

A. Adler and C. Furtmüller, *Heilen und Bilden* (1916)

E. Bleuler, *Physisch und Psychisch in der Pathologie* (1916)

L. Kaplan, *Psychoanalytische Probleme* (1916)

J. J. Putnam, *The Work of Adler* (1917)

J. H. Schultz, *Freuds Sexualpsychoanalyse* (1917)

E. Claparède, *Rêve satisfaisant un désir organique* (1917)

J. Schaxel, *Über die Darstellung allgemeiner Biologie* (1919)

A. Lipschütz, *Die Pubertätsdrüse und ihre Wirkungen* (1920)

O. Gross, *Drei Aufsätze über den inneren Konflikt* (1920)

S. Freud, *Drei Abhandlungen zur Sexualtheorie* (4th edition, 1921)

K. Abraham, *Klinische Beiträge zur Psychoanalyse* (1922)

R. de Saussure, *La méthode psychanalytique* (1922)

Note: the author plans to co-ordinate a translation and edition of these unpublished texts to form a fourth English volume of Ferenczi's work.

GENERAL WORKS

All books are published in London unless otherwise indicated.

Abraham, K. (1954) *Selected Papers on Psycho-Analysis*, D. Bryan and A. Strachey, trans. Hogarth.

—— (1955) *Clinical Papers and Essays on Psycho-Analysis*, H. Abraham and D. R. Ellison, trans. Hogarth.

—— et al. ([1919] 1921) *Psycho-Analysis and the War Neuroses.* International Psycho-Analytic Press.

Abraham, N. and Torok, M. (1976) *Cryptonymie: le verbier de l'homme aux loups.* Paris: Aubier Flammarion.

Adler, A. (1912) *Über den nervösen Charakter.* Frankfurt am Main: Fischer, 1972.

—— (1929) *The Practice and Theory of Individual Psychology,* P. Radin, trans. Kegan Paul.

Aichorn, A. (1925) *Verwahrloste Jugend.* Vienna: Internationaler Psychoanalytischer Verlag.

—— (1964) *Delinquency and Child Guidance: Selected Papers.* O. Fleischmann, P. Kramer and H. Ross, eds New York: International Universities Press.

—— (1976) *Wer war August Aichorn.* Vienna: Löcker & Wögenstein.

Alexander, F. (1933) 'On Ferenczi's relaxation principle', *Int. J. Psycho-Anal.* 14(2):183–92.

—— (1956) 'Two forms of regression and their therapeutic implications', *Psychoanal.* 25.

—— (1960) *Fundamentals of Psychoanalysis.* Allen & Unwin.

Balint, M. (1949) 'Sándor Ferenczi', *Int. J. Psycho-Anal.* 30.

—— (1952) *Primary Love and Psycho-Analytic Technique.* Hogarth.

—— (1956) *Problems of Human Pleasure and Behaviour.* New York: Liveright.

—— (1957) *The Doctor, his Patient, and the Illness.* Pitman.

—— (1959) *Thrills and Regressions.* Hogarth.

—— (1967) 'Sándor Ferenczi's technical experiments', in B. Wolman, ed. *Psychoanalytic Techniques.* New York: Basic, pp. 147–67.

—— (1968) *The Basic Fault.* Tavistock.

Barande, I. (1972). *Sándor Ferenczi.* Paris: Payot.

Bentovim, A. *et al.* (1989) *Child Sexual Abuse within the Family: Assessment and Treatment.* Wright.

Bernheimer, C. and Kahane, C., eds (1985) *In Dora's Case.* Virago.

Bion, W. (1967) *Second Thoughts.* Heinemann.

Bjerre, P. (1911) '*Zur Radikalbehandlung der chronischen Para-noia*', *Jahrbuch*, 3(2).

―――― (1914) '*Das Wesen der Hypnose*', *Zeitschrift für Psychotherapie und medizinische Psychologie* 4(1) April.

Bourguignon, A., Cotet, P., Laplanche, J. and Robert, F. (1989) *Traduire Freud*. Paris: PUF.

Brabant, E. (1990) *Histoire du Mouvement Psychanalytique Hongrois*. Paris: PUF.

Brouardel, P. (1883) *Des causes d'erreur dans les expertises relatives aux attentats à la pudeur*. Paris: Baillière.

Burnet, E. M. (1952) 'Recovery from a long neurosis', *Psychiatry* 15(2) May.

―――― (1954) 'Sándor Ferenczi', *Psychiatric Quarterly Supplement*.

Carotenuto, A. (1982) *A Secret Symmetry: Sabina Spielrein Between Jung and Freud*. New York: Random House.

Chasseguet-Smirgel, J. (1967) '*À propos de la technique active de Ferenczi*', in *Pour une psychanalyse de l'art et de la créativité*. Paris: Payot.

Cremerius, J. (1983) '*Die Sprache der Zärtlichkeit und der Leidenschaft. Reflexionen zu Sándor Ferenczi Vortrag von 1932*', *Psyché* 37.

Dadoun, R. (1972) *Géza Roheim*. Paris: Payot.

de Forest, I. (1954) *The Leaven of Love: The Development of the Psychoanalytic Theory and Technique of Sándor Ferenczi*. New York: Harper.

Derrida, J. (1980) *La carte postale de Socrate à Freud et au-delà*. Paris: Flammarion.

DSM-III (1987) *The Diagnostic and Statistical Manual of Mental Disorders*, third edition - revised. Washington, DC: American Psychiatric Association.

Dupont, J. (1988) 'Introduction', in *The Clinical Diary of Sándor Ferenczi*. Cambridge, MA: Harvard University Press.

Eissler, K. (1982) *Freud as an Expert Witness: The Discussion of War Neuroses between Freud and Wagner-Jauregg*. New York: International Universities Press, 1986.

English, H. B. and A. C. (1958) *A Comprehensive Dictionary of Psychological and Psychoanalytic Terms*. Heinemann.

Fallend, K. (1988) *Wilhelm Reich in Wien: Psychoanalyse und Politik*. Salzburg: Geyer.

Falzeder, E. (1986) *Die 'Sprachverwirrung' und die 'Grundstorung'*. Salzburg: Salzburg.

Freud, S. (1953–1974) *The Standard Edition of the Complete Psychological Works of Sigmund Freud*, under the general editorship of James Strachey in collaboration with Anna Freud, assisted by Alix Strachey and Alan Tyson, 24 volumes, Hogarth. Note: numbers following references in the text denote the volume concerned (e.g. *The Interpretation of Dreams* [1900a] [Freud, 4, p. 213] refers to volume 4 of the *Standard Edition*, page 213).

—————— (1915) *A Phylogenetic Fantasy: Overview of the Transference Neuroses*, I. Grubrich-Simitis, ed., A. and P. T. Hoffer, trans. Cambridge, MA: Harvard University Press, 1987.

—————— (1924) 'Sándor Ferenczi', *Int. J. Psycho-Anal.* 14: 207.

—————— and Fliess, W. (1985) *The Complete Letters of Sigmund Freud to Wilhelm Fliess 1887–1904*, J. Masson, trans. and ed. Cambridge, MA: Harvard University Press.

—————— and Jung, C. G. (1974) *The Freud/Jung letters*, W. McGuire, ed., R. Mannheim and R. F. C. Hull, trans. Hogarth and Routledge.

Fromm, E. (1963) *The Dogma of Christ*. Routledge & Kegan Paul.

Gay, P. (1988) *Freud. A Life for Our Time*. Dent.

Gedo, J. (1976) 'The wise baby reconsidered', in J. Gedo and G. H. Pollock, eds. *Freud: The Fusion of Science and Humanism – The Intellectual History of Psychoanalysis*. New York: International Universities Press.

Glover, E. (1955) *The Technique of Psycho-Analysis*. New York: International Universities Press.

—————— and Brierley, M. J. (1940) *An Investigation of the Technique of Psycho-Analysis*. Baillière.

Gould, S. J. (1984) *Ontogeny and Phylogeny*. Cambridge, MA: Harvard University Press.

Groddeck, G. (1917) *Die psychische Bedingtheit und psychoanalytische Behandlung organischer Leiden.* Berlin: Hirzel.

—— (1921) *Der Seelensucher: ein psychoanalytischer Roman.* Vienna: Imago 7.

—— (1923) *The Book of the It: Psychoanalytic Letters to a Friend.* Daniel, 1935.

Gross, O. (1909) *Über psychopathologische Minderwertigkeiten.* Vienna: Halle.

Grosskurth, P. (1985) *Melanie Klein: Her World and Her Work.* Hodder; Karnac/Maresfield, 1986.

Grunberger, B. (1974) 'De la technique active à la confusion de langues', *Revue française de psychanalyse* 38: 521–46.

Harmat, P. (1988) *Freud, Ferenczi, und die ungarische Psychoanalyse.* Tübingen: Diskord.

Haynal, A. (1988) *The Technique at Issue: Controversies in Psychoanalysis from Freud and Ferenczi to Michael Balint.* Karnac.

Hermann, I. (1946) 'Report on the Hungarian Psycho-Analytical Society', *Int. J. Psycho-Anal.* 27: 87–92.

—— (1953) 'Die Objektivität in Jones' Diagnose über Ferenczis Krankheit', *Psyché* 7.

Hillman, J. (1972) *The Myth of Analysis.* Evanston, IL: Northwestern University Press.

—— (1975) *Re-Visioning Psychology.* New York: Harper.

—— (1985) *Anima: An Anatomy of a Personified Notion.* Dallas, TX: Spring.

—— and Boer, C. (1985) *Freud's own Cookbook.* New York: Harper.

Hinshelwood, R. D. (1989) *A Dictionary of Kleinian Thought.* Free Association Books.

Hirschfeld, M. (1959) *Sexual Anomalies and Perversions: Physical and Psychological Development, Diagnosis, and Treatment.* Sidders.

Hitschmann, E. (1921) *Freud's Theories of the Neuroses.* Kegan Paul.

Hoensch, J. K. (1988) *A History of Modern Hungary 1867–1986,* K. Traynor, trans. Longman.

Hollos, I. (1928) *Hinter der gelben Mauer. Von der Befreiung des Irren.* Stuttgart, Leipzig, Zürich: Hippokrates.

Irigaray, L. (1974) *Speculum de l'autre femme.* Paris: Minuit.

—— (1979) *Et l'une ne bouge pas sans l'autre.* Paris: Minuit.

—— (1982) *Passions élémentaires.* Paris: Minuit.

—— (1987) *Sexes et parentés.* Paris: Minuit.

—— (1989) *Le temps de la différence.* Librairie générale française.

Jacoby, R. (1983) *The Repression of Psychoanalysis.* New York: Basic.

Janet, P. (1898) *Névroses et idées fixes,* 2 volumes. Paris: Alcan.

—— (1907) *The Major Symptoms of Hysteria.* Macmillan.

Jones, E. (1953/1957) *Sigmund Freud: Life and Work,* 3 volumes. Hogarth.

—— (1959) *Free Associations: Memories of a Psychoanalyst.* New York: Basic.

Jung, C. G. (1919) *Psychology of the Unconscious,* B. M. Hinkle, trans. Routledge.

—— (1972/1983) *The Collected Works of C. G. Jung,* 18 volumes, 1 supplementary volume 'The Zofingia Lectures', H. Read, M. Fordham and G. Adler, eds, L. Stein and R. F. C. Hull, trans. Note: references in the text are followed by the volume number: for example, *The Psychology of Dementia Praecox* [*1907*], (Jung, 3, p. 65) refers to volume 3, page 65.

Karsch-Haack, F. (1911) *Das gleichgeschlechtliche Leben der Naturvölker.* Munich: Reinhardt.

Kestenberg, J. (1975) *Children and Parents: Psychoanalytic Studies in Development.* New York: Aronson.

Klein, M. (1932) *Die Psychoanalyse des Kindes.* Vienna: Internationaler Psychoanalytischer Verlag.

—— (1975) *The Writings of Melanie Klein,* 4 volumes: 1 *Love, Guilt and Reparation;* 2 *The Psycho-Analysis of Children;* 3 *Envy and Gratitude;* 4 *Narrative of a Child Analysis.* Hogarth and the Institute of Psycho-Analysis.

Kovacs, V. (1935) '*Lehranalyse und Kontrollanalyse*', *Zeitschrift* 21: 517–24.

Kropotkin, P. (1902) *Mutual Aid: A Factor in Evolution.* Heinemann.

Krzowski, S. and Land, P. (1988) *In Our Experience: Workshops at the Women's Therapy Centre.* Women's Press.

Lacan, J. (1966) *Écrits.* Paris: Seuil.

—— (1977) *Ecrits – A Selection,* A. Sheridan, trans. Tavistock.

LaCapra, D. (1988) 'History and psychoanalysis', in F. Meltzer, ed. *The Trial (s) of Psychoanalysis.* Chicago: Chicago University Press, pp. 9–38.

Laplanche, J. (1970) *Vie et mort en psychanalyse.* Paris: Flammarion.

—— (1980/87) *Problématiques,* 5 volumes. Paris: PUF.

—— (1989) *New foundations for Psychoanalysis,* D. Macey, trans. Oxford: Blackwell.

—— and Pontalis, J. B. (1980) *The Language of Psycho-Analysis,* D. Nicholson-Smith, trans. Hogarth.

Lieberman, E. J. (1985) *Acts of Will: The Life and Work of Otto Rank.* New York: Free Press.

Lorin, C. (1983) *Le jeune Ferenczi.* Paris: Aubier.

McCaffrey, P. (1989) *Freud and Dora: The Artful Dream.* New Brunswick, NJ: Rutgers University Press.

Mahler, M. (1988) *The Memoirs of Margaret Mahler,* P. Stepansky, ed. New York: Free Press.

Mahoney, P. (1984) *Cries of the Wolf Man.* New Haven, CT: Yale University Press.

—— (1987) *Freud as Writer.* New Haven, CT: Yale University Press.

Masson, J. (1984) *The Assault on Truth.* Faber.

—— (1989) *Against Therapy.* Collins.

Meltzer, D. (1978) *The Kleinian Development.* Strath and Perthshire: Clunie.

Menaker, E. (1982) *Otto Rank – A Rediscovered Legacy.* New York: Columbia University Press.

Merskey, H. (1979) *The Analysis of Hysteria.* Baillière.

Miller, A. (1985) *Thou Shalt Not Be Aware.* Pluto.

Miller, G. (1975) 'Crime et suggestion', *Ornicar?* 4:27–80.

Myers, F. W. H. (1935) *Human Personality and its Survival of Bodily Death*. Longman.

Ornston, D. (1982) 'Strachey's influence: a preliminary report', *Int. J. Psycho-Anal.* 63: 409–26.

Palmier, J. M. (1982) '*La psychanalyse en Hongrie*', in R. Jaccard, ed. *Histoire de la psychanalyse*, vol 2. Paris: Hachette, pp. 145–86.

Pontalis, J. B. (1968) *Après Freud*. Paris: Gallimard.

Putnam, J. J. (1971) *James Jackson Putnam and Psychoanalysis: Letters between Putnam and Freud, Jones, William James, Sándor Ferenczi, and Morton Prince 1877–1917*, N. G. Hale, ed. Cambridge, MA: Harvard University Press.

Quinn, S. (1988) *A Mind of Her Own: The Life of Karen Horney*. Macmillan.

Rank, O. (1929) *The Trauma of Birth*. Routledge.

—— (1971) *The Double*. New York: New American Library.

—— (1975) *The Don Juan Legend*, D. Winter, trans. Princeton, NJ: Princeton University Press.

Reich, W. (1925) *Der Triebhafte Charakter*, B. Koopman, trans. as *The Impulsive Character and Other Essays*, New York: New American Library, 1974.

—— (1929/34) *Sex-Pol* (*Essays 1929–1934*), L. Baxandall, ed. New York: Random, 1966.

—— (1933) *Character Analysis*. New York: Pocket, 1976.

Revardel, J. L. (1986) '*Analogies à propos de Thalassa*', *Le coq-héron* 98: 55–60.

Riviere, J. (1937) 'Hate, greed, and aggression', in *Love, Hate and Reparation*, M. Klein and J. Riviere, eds. Hogarth.

Roazen, P. (1979) *Freud and His Followers*. Harmondsworth: Penguin.

Sabourin, P. (1985) *Ferenczi, Paladin et Grand Vizir Secret*. Paris: Éditions Universitaires.

Schmideberg, M. (1935) 'Reassurance as a means of analytic technique', *Int. J. Psycho-Anal.* 16: 307–24.

Severn, E. (1913) *Psychotherapy: Its Doctrine and Practice*. Rider.

—— (1920) *The Psychology of Behaviour: A Practical Study of*

Human Personality and Conduct with Special Reference to Methods of Development. Paul.

—— (1933) *The Discovery of the Self: A Study of Psychological Cure.* Rider.

Sharaf, M. (1983) *Fury on Earth: A Biography of Wilhelm Reich.* Deutsch.

Silberer, H. (1970) *Problems of Mysticism and its Symbolism.* New York: Weiser.

Simitis, I. (1981) '*Sigmund Freud/Sándor Ferenczi: Sechs Briefe zur Wechselbeziehungen von psychoanalytischer Theorie und Technik*', in G. Jappe and C. Nedelmann, eds. *Zur Psychoanalyse der Objektbeziehungen*, Problemata Fromann-Holzboog, 88.

Sontag, S. (1977) *Illness as Metaphor.* Harmondsworth: Penguin.

—— (1989) *AIDS and its Metaphors.* Harmondsworth: Penguin.

Spielrein, S. (1912) '*Die Destruktion als Ursache des Werdens*', *Jahrbuch für psychoanalytische und psychopathologische Forschungen* 4: 465–503.

—— (1922) '*Die Entstehung der kindlichen Worte Papa und Mama*', *Imago* 8: 345–67.

Stanton, K. (1988) 'Temples or prisons', *Times Higher Educational Supplement* 26.

—— and Stanton, M. (1989) 'Martha Davis: non-verbal aspects of psychotherapy', *Bulletin of the Royal College of Psychiatrists*, July 1989.

Stanton, M. (1988) 'Wilhelm Stekel: a refugee analyst and his English reception', in E. Timms and N. Segal, eds. *Freud in Exile.* New Haven, CT: Yale University Press, pp. 163–74.

—— (1991) '*Laissez-faire*: James Strachey and Freud's French', *Int. Rev. Psycho-Anal.* 18(1).

Steiner, G. (1978) 'A remark on language and psychoanalysis', in *On Difficulty and Other Essays.* Oxford University Press.

Sterba, R. F. (1982) *Reminiscences of a Viennese Psychoanalyst.* Detroit, MI: Wayne State University.

—— (1987) 'The psychic trauma and the handling of the transference (the last contributions of Sandor Ferenczi to psychoanalytic technique)', in *Richard Sterba: The Collected Papers*, H. Daldin, ed. New York: North River Press.

Sulloway, F. (1979) *Freud, Biologist of the Mind.* Fontana.

Tardieu, A. (1852–4) *Dictionnaire d'hygiène publique et de salubrité,* 3 volumes. Paris: Baillière.

This, B. (1986) '*La direction de la cure et Ferenczi*', *Le coq-heron* 98: 52–4.

Thompson, C. (1943) 'The therapeutic technique of Sándor Ferenczi', *Int. J. Psycho-Anal.* 24: 64–6.

—— (1950) *Psychoanalysis: Evolution and Development.* New York: Grove.

Thornton, E. M. (1983) *Freud and Cocaine: The Freudian Fallacy.* Blond & Briggs.

Timms, E. and Segal, N., eds. (1988) *Freud in Exile.* New Haven, CT: Yale University Press.

Torok, M. (1984) '*La correspondance Freud–Ferenczi*', *Confrontations,* autumn issue, 12.

Vahinger, H. (1897) *The Philosophy of 'As If'.* Routledge & Kegan Paul, 1935.

Völgyes, I., ed. (1971) *Hungary in Revolution 1918–1919.* Lincoln, Nebraska: University of Nebraska Press.

Winnicott, D. W. (1949) 'Mind and its relation to the psyche-soma', in *Through Paediatrics to Psycho-Analysis.* Hogarth, 1987.

—— (1971) *Playing and Reality.* Tavistock.

Wolman, B., ed. (1967) *Psychoanalytic Techniques.* New York: Basic.

Young-Bruehl, E. (1988) *Anna Freud.* Macmillan.

Index

This first edition of
Stanton's Sándor Ferenczi
was finished in May 1991.

The book was commissioned and edited
by Robert M. Young,
copy-edited by Gillian Wilce,
indexed by Martin Stanton,
designed by Wendy Millichap,
and produced by Adelle Krauser
for Free Association Books and Jason
Aronson, Inc.